T TLAND

"CHIEF OF THE BIG MOUNTAIN"

[The Governor-General of Canada, *alias* Lord Tweedsmuir, *alias* Mr. John Buchan, has just received the above honorific title from a Red Indian Tribe.]

By kind permission of Punch

THE KIRK IN SCOTLAND

JOHN BUCHAN

With a postscript by R. D. Kernohan

LABARUM PUBLICATIONS LTD.
DUNBAR

Published 1985 by Labarum Publications Ltd.,
The Abbey, Dunbar

First published by Hodder & Stoughton Ltd. in 1930

ISBN 0–948095–00–8 p/b
ISBN 0–948095–01–6 h/b

Printed in Great Britain by
McCorquodale (Scotland) Ltd.

CONTENTS

CONTENTS (continued)

INTRODUCTION

This chapter is not an essay in Church history. History is an ampler thing which demands exact documentation and a multitude of details. It is no more than an attempt to sketch on the broadest lines the career of the Church in Scotland; the vicissitudes which it suffered from controversies within and without its bounds; the different strands interwoven in its creed; the slow stages by which it attained to a clearer consciousness of its nature and its destiny.

I write as one who believes that that Church throughout its history was divinely inspired, and never in its darkest days ceased to fulfil in some degree its high mission.

But I believe, too, that, since it was also a human institution officered by fallible men, it blundered often, and had many needless years of sojourning in the wilderness. If the spark of celestial origin did not wholly die, other fires burned fiercely which were not divinely kindled. Yet it seems to me that we can discern a real continuity of growth. Slowly, very slowly, it discovered that comprehension was only possible if combined with tolerance. Through difficult stages it moved to a simplification of its confessions, and learned to distinguish essentials from "circumstantials." It became more clearly aware of the precise nature of its mission, and therefore of its proper relation to the civil government of the State. Without this steady simplifying and purifying process which its history reveals, the union of to-day would have been unthinkable. I am not of those who believe that true progress is ever attained by a straight and easy road, and beyond doubt the Church in Scotland has had to contend for every step of its advance. But it seems to me that, in spite of " right-hand snares and extremes and left-hand way-slidings," its story reveals, as in a spiral, a continuous upward movement.

There is no lack of literature on the subject, but the reader may find himself in trouble if he plunges without guidance into its mazes. Much of it is uncritical and unhistorical. The chronicle of the Scottish Church has too often been compiled in the spirit of hagiography. Some writers have approached it in a mood of rapt exaltation, and produced a device in snow and ink—spotless saints and infallible wisdom set against scowling diabolists and malignant folly. There has been no lack of casuists to defend the indefensible. It may be fairly said that history conceived in such a spirit does scant justice to the Church itself. On the other hand, it is easy for the cynic so to set forth its disputes as to make them seem the merest logomachies. The old divines write often uncouth English, and they are apt to make their arguments a mosaic of Scripture texts which lends itself readily to caricature. Causes for which men freely offered their lives can be made to seem trivial or ridiculous.

Of the two faults I think this the worse, for it is the less intelligent. The blindest hagiology seems to me preferable to that detachment which never comes within measurable distance of the point. Knox, Melville and Henderson—Boyd, Durham and Rutherford—Boston and the Erskines—Chalmers, Cunningham and Candlish—all were men of remarkable gifts of character and mind ; we may fairly assume that they did not give their time to wrangling about trifles ; it is our business to find out what kernel of living truth is concealed in a language which may have passed out of use. We must approach the historical Church with some equipment in the way of historical imagination, for even in its blunders we may find enlightenment. We cannot afford to look scornfully on any belief which once "taught weak wills how much they can." And there is this reward for the honest inquirer. Without some understanding of the Church there can be no true understanding of Scottish history or of the nature of the Scottish people.

I

The Mediaeval Church

The Church in Scotland has a long ancestry, but its descent is not in direct line. The Christian faith was first brought to our shores towards the end of the fourth century, when Ninian settled at Whithorn and built a great white church to the glory of God and the memory of St. Martin of Tours ; but soon the tides of war and paganism flowed over his work. In the middle of the sixth century Kentigern became the apostle of

Strathclyde, and, as St. Mungo, the patron saint of Glasgow. On Whit Sunday in the year 563 Columba landed in Iona, and he made that isle for the remaining thirty-four years of his life a light, the beams of which shone over all Scotland. We must give up, I fear, the pleasant tale derived from John of Fordun, of the early Scottish Church as being in substance Presbyterian and non-Roman. That Church was, like the Irish Church, monastic in its structure ; but as soon as it becomes an organised and national institution it is part of the catholic European system, though monastic elements, like the Culdees, long remain to testify to its beginnings.

It is as unhistorical to picture an early anti-papal Scottish Church as to imagine that the niceties of Roman rule were from the first universal, or that the Middle Ages knew only one uniform ecclesiastical pattern. There was nationalism in every Church ; most sovereigns had their quarrels with the

Pope, and many peoples lay occasionally under his ban. In Britain there was, perhaps, a special degree of spiritual independence. James I. of Scotland, a devout son of the Church, was as ready to assert himself against undue papal interference as William the Conqueror. The Scot, indeed, when he travelled abroad, carried with him a certain flavour of heterodoxy, and the validity of his orders was sometimes questioned. But in general we may say that the mediaeval Scottish Church was a normal branch of the Church Catholic whose centre was Rome.

It has been the fashion ever since the Reformation to picture that Church in dark colours, as something alien and despotic, with small hold on the affections of the people. The view has little warrant. The questioning spirit of the nation sometimes set the popular mind against its own hierarchy, and more often against the Roman Pontiff, for the Scot has always been more individualist than catholic, and his aspiration that of the old song :

> That all the world shall see
> There 's nane right but we,
> The men of the auld Scottish nation.

But the mediaeval Church gave to the people all of religion and humane learning that they knew, and there is ample evidence that it played, even in its decadence, a vital part in men's lives. It produced the only sacred poetry of the highest class that Scotland can claim. From the earliest days it had its reformers and its evangelists as well as its moderates. Even at the Reformation the Christian virtues were not all on one side. The great churchmen were often, like Lamberton and Wishart, leaders in the fight for national independence. Henry Wardlaw who founded the University of St. Andrews, Kennedy who succeeded him in that see, William Turnbull to whom we owe the University of Glasgow, William Elphinstone who was the creator of King's College at Aberdeen, must rank high amongst the benefactors of their country.

The Church which had endured for nearly a thousand years disappeared almost in a night, and with it went, unhappily, most of the outward evidence of its existence. Few ancient buildings remain still in use to remind us of that vanished world. But if we lack such memorials, we may claim an ultimate shrine. If the stream of Church history seems to be long lost among sands and morasses, we can recognise its fount. The little isle with its green hills and white beaches, which looks across the ribbon of tide to the granite of Mull, is a sacred place to which the devotion of every Scottish creed and communion is vowed. For there Columba, warrior, saint, scholar, explorer and law-giver, taught a simple evangel, first to the Gael and then to the other peoples of the mainland, and thereby lit the lamp of a missionary faith which has flickered often, but has never died. Iona is the Holy Land and the Holy City of Scotland, the spring of "the wisdom before which knowledge is as a frosty breath."

II

The First Reformation

The Reformation came to Scotland in its most drastic form. There remained indeed the same major articles of the Christian faith, but, on grounds partly political and partly religious, there was a final breach with Rome, to some extent in creed and to the full in ritual and Church government. It began with the "Band" of December 1557, which denounced Roman abuses and demanded the English Prayer-book: in August 1560 a Confession of Faith, drawn up by John Knox and his friends, was ratified by Parliament as "wholesome and sound doctrine grounded upon the infallible truth of God's word" ; a few months later the first General Assembly was held, and the First Book of Discipline was approved ; and in the December Parliament of 1567, during the regency of Moray, the reformed Church was established by a statute " declaring and granting jurisdiction " to it, and disallowing " any other face of Kirk in Scotland."

The keynote of the Reformation was a return to simplicity. The great structure of the mediaeval Church, with its accretions of fifteen centuries, was exchanged for a simple revelation—God speaking through His Word to the individual heart and judgment. It claimed to replace an external standard by an internal, to be a re-birth of the spirit of man and a vindication of the liberties of the human soul. Its fundamental doctrine was the priesthood of all believers. Its conception of the Church was of a free autonomous community owning no leadership but that of Jesus Christ. But, since a human institution cannot be founded upon the bare principle of liberty, the new Church was at once compelled to seek definition and discipline.

The Reformation in its extremest, or, if we prefer, its purest form, was mainly the work of John Calvin, who performed two tasks of the first importance. In his *Institutes* he codified the theology of St. Augustine, and provided a body of doctrine, differing, indeed, only in emphasis from Catholic dogma, but skilfully adapted to the new conditions. In the Church which he founded at Geneva he created a model which Knox thought " the most perfect School of Christ that ever was on earth since the days of the Apostles," and which had a profound influence upon the nascent Church in Scotland.

But the hardening of the molten ore of spiritual fervour in the moulds of an institution was attended with certain difficulties, and, since in them is to be found the germ of all the later troubles of the

Scottish Church, it is necessary to examine them with some care.

The Basis of Faith

(1) The first concerned the basis of faith. The foundation of the Reformed Churches was the Bible ; they accepted no truth which had not a Scriptural warrant, and they claimed that whatever they did was done by Scripture authority. But the Bible must be interpreted, and the only means of interpretation, once the authority of an infallible Church had been rejected, was the human judgment and the human conscience. That remained the view of the more liberal among the Reformed theologians. " The authority of man," Hooker wrote, " is the key which openeth the door of entrance into the knowledge of the Scriptures."

But such a view inevitably involved diversity of opinion, and it seemed an insecure basis on which to build a lasting fabric.

Luther and Zwingli, for example, both founding upon the Bible, had reached different conclusions about the meaning of the Eucharist. Calvin and those who followed him saw the danger, and endeavoured to avoid it by something very like a return to the ecclesiasticism which he had rejected. We know, he held, that the Bible is the Word of God, not because of the authority of an historic Church, but because of the testimony of the Holy Spirit. This testimony must be systematised by God's servants, and a Church erected which shall be the medium of the Holy Spirit and the treasury of inspired interpretation. His *Institutes* in their second edition made definite claim to be the canon of Scripture teaching ; it was in his new Church and its accepted creed that saving knowledge could alone be found. This was not far from that doctrine of an external, infallible canon which the earlier Reformers had rejected.

Such an attitude towards the Bible and its

interpretation was a fruitful parent of strife. In the first place, it led to the most forced and arbitrary reading of Scripture texts. The Bible was made the sole manual of practice. The Church of Calvin and Knox forgot the warning of St. Paul—that the Old Testament was a dangerous book if the letter of it was regarded to the exclusion of the spirit, and it tended to make it a storehouse of minute precedents. The Roman Church had used for its basis not the Bible only, but the writings of the Fathers, and the dictates of practical experience, and it possessed the power of regulating the whole, and providing for natural development, by authoritative decree. The Scottish Church retained this doctrine of authority, but had somehow to harmonise it with a quantum of individual liberty, and it narrowed the canon to the two Testaments, thereby perilously limiting its tools.

At the beginning there was indeed a certain laxity. In 1558 the Scottish Protestants petitioned Mary of Guise that all matters might be tried by the New Testament, the ancient Fathers, and the "godly laws of Justinian." Knox, when it suited him, was prepared to differ even from the New Testament, and in an argument with Maitland of Lethington, who quoted St. James's direction to St. Paul to purify himself in the Temple, was bold enough to doubt "whether either James's command or Paul's obedience proceeded from the Holy Ghost." When Alexander Henderson disputed with Charles I., and the King argued that, when the Bible was not explicit, it was right to have recourse to the records of the Church, Henderson met him fairly on his own ground. But in general the early history of the Scottish Church shows a steady hardening and narrowing in its apologetics.

From this constriction of basis many misfortunes were to flow. The first was a perpetual risk of heresy and a constant invitation to schism. If ancient writings were to be construed without scientific method or historical perspective, it was certain that human ingenuity would find many causes of division. A second was the ossification of the minds engaged in so barren a task. The human reason in its worthier sense was atrophied by being limited to a futile casuistry. Superstitions, such as witchcraft and demoniac possession, were given by the idolatry of the Old Testament a new lease of life. The free use of the intellect was paralysed, and honest men become sophists. Ninian Winzet in his controversy with Knox had no difficulty in showing that the Reformers went to the Bible to find proofs for their creed, not to find that creed, since they rejected certain rules of the Roman Church which had scriptural warrant, and accepted others which had none. Andrew Melville based his objection to bishops on the ground that in the New Testament there was no mention of bishops ruling over presbyteries, ignoring the fact that his own system had just as little warrant, since there was no proof of a presbytery governing more than a single church.

In the following century the attitude became still more rigid. One Johann Koch of Leyden became, as Cocceius, anathema to the orthodox, because he held the reasonable view that Hebrew sentences should be interpreted by their context. Spiritually and intellectually this searching for proof-texts became a disease, for the truth in Donne's saying was ignored, that "sentences in Scripture, like hairs in horses' tails, concur in one root of beauty and strength, but, being plucked out one by one, serve only for springes and snares." Considerations of expediency and common sense were banned: the Bible was made a handbook to every aspect of life; no word of the sacred writings but was regarded as dogma; every syllable, letter, comma and full-stop was treated as divinely inspired: whatever was not contained therein was unlawful, for it was laid down as the first principle of interpretation that for God not to command was to forbid. And so we have Samuel Rutherford in his *Divine Right of Church Government and Excommunication* declaring that " there is nothing so small in either doctrinals or policy, so as man may alter, omit, or leave off these smallest positive things that God hath commanded."

This passionate formalism must obviously lead to credal divergencies, and it must inevitably land a Church in difficulties about rites and ceremonies. It was not easy to accommodate Christian worship in Western Europe in the sixteenth century to the practice of Judaean peasants in the first, or of Israel a thousand years earlier. The immediate result was confusion. The early Reformers in Scotland had no objection to settled forms and prescribed prayers. Knox began by accepting the kneeling posture at communion, though he afterwards rejected it. Wafer bread was employed by Calvin in his own church at Geneva. Winzet pointed out to Knox that there was no explicit warrant in the New Testament for either the baptism of infants or the strict observance of the Lord's Day. The first Reformers derived from the Church they had left a preference for a certain catholic order in worship until they were overborne by the Scripture literalists. This influence came chiefly from the English Puritans; under their guidance Sunday, the day on which Calvin had played at bowls and Knox had given supper-parties, became the Jewish Sabbath, and selections from the Mosaic law were dovetailed into the Christian creed. Even the ring in marriage would have been abolished had not the women proved stronger than the preachers.

The Conception of the Church

(2) If the seeds of dissension lay hidden in a basis of faith too narrow for the human

spirit, they were also present in the new conception of the Church. Presbytery, being based on the Word of God, was a system *divini juris* ; its founders were possessed by the mediaeval idea of a universal Church ; therefore we find it speedily claiming the right to insist upon religious uniformity. It was not only divinely founded, but, with its Continental analogues, was the only system of divine origin. It is easy to see how such an attitude came about, for against the universal claim of Rome it seemed necessary to establish a counter-universalism. But it involved two dangerous consequences—the prohibition of variety in religious belief and usage, and the duty of coercion. To the Scottish Reformers it appeared that no religion was safe unless it were predominant.

The new Church held firm by the Catholic doctrine of comprehension, but it insisted also upon uniformity—an apparently irreconcilable ideal. The Church of Rome had permitted within its pale all who formally assented to its creed ; the Reformers tended to make the " church visible " also the " church invisible." The classic authority is the sixteenth chapter of Knox's *Confession* :

> " As we believe in one God, Father, Son and Holy Ghost, so do we most constantly believe that from the beginning there hath been, now is, and to the end of the world shall be, one Kirk ; that is to say, one company and multitude of men chosen of God, who rightly worship and embrace him by true faith in Christ Jesus . . . which kirk is Catholic, that is, universal, because it containeth the elect of all realms, nations and tongues. And we utterly abhor the blasphemy of those that affirm that men which live according to equity and justice shall be saved, what religion soever they have professed."

The practical doctrine, adumbrated by Knox and made explicit by his successors, was that it was God's will that the Kirk, which was scripturally the only true Kirk, should admit no rival in any sphere where it had won dominance, and should suffer no internal divergencies from its divinely-inspired interpretation of Scriptural mandates. It believed, as Rome believed, in the ideal of a single Church, a complete and exclusive system to which a single separatist was anathema.

From such a conception the duty of coercion inevitably followed. Our Lord never taught the exercise of coercive power, and the early Church was not in a position to attempt it. But in the fourth century, with the acknowledgment of Christianity as the State religion, the practice began; heresy became treason; and St. Augustine, building on the isolated text, "Compel them to come in," preached the use of force in conversion. The view was based upon his doctrine of the utter depravity of the natural man, since, if human nature was hopelessly corrupt, there was no reason to consult its wishes. "What can be more deadly to the soul," he asked, "than the liberty of error?" "Toleration," said Richard Baxter in the seventeenth century, " is soul murder." The view was inevitable, granted the premises, for on them tolerance seemed no better than spiritual sloth and moral apathy. This was the belief alike of Protestant and Catholic, of Knox and of Innocent III., of Andrew Melville and of the Cardinal of Lorraine. A man like Samuel Rutherford, who was what was commonly known as an " affectionate " preacher, taught, as has been said, " the loveliness of Christ for thirty years without ever perceiving the unloveliness of intolerance."

Another consequence was the institution of a drastic internal discipline, in order that the visible might be made to approximate as far as possible to the invisible Church. Evidence, indeed, could not be demanded of the possession of saving grace, but over every outward manifestation there was exercised a minute inquisition. No serious attempt was made to distinguish between moral fundamentals and non-fundamentals, and the most secular aspects of life were not exempted from oversight. Once again the conclusion followed logically from certain dubious premises. Historically we can perceive its justification, but in its results it was disastrous. "By your hard and subtle words," Cromwell was to tell the ministers before Dunbar, "you have begotten prejudice in those who do too much in matters of conscience—wherein every soul has to answer for itself to God—depend upon you"; and the indictment was unhappily true.

The Relation to the Civil Power

(3) The third potential source of strife was the relation to the civil power. Ever since Constantine this problem had confronted the Church, and the great *Corpus Juris* of Justinian defined the respective rights of Church and State—a definition at first accepted by the Reformers. Presently their attitude changed. Hag-ridden by Old

Testament precedents, they came to believe that the visible sign of God's acknowledgment of His people was the gift of political power. The Church was not only supreme in spiritual matters, but it was the duty of a Christian State to support it and to lend the secular arm, when required, to carry out its decrees, to punish heresy and enforce discipline, and to suppress any Church which threatened rivalry. In the fathers of Presbytery there was nothing of the *politique* whose creed has been defined by Tavannes : " Ceux qui preférent le repos du royaume, ou de leur particulier, au salut de leur âme, et à la religion, qui ayment mieux que le royaume demeure en paix sans Dieu qu'en guerre pour luy." [1]

This view involved the Church's establishment, and Knox and Melville and Henderson were Erastians in one sense of that doubtful word. Moreover, the rejection of toleration and the belief in uniformity were

[1] *Mémoires*, ed. Buchon, 269.

bound to lead to a usurpation of civil power. With such a creed there could be no real delimitation between the spiritual and the secular, between Church and State. The right of the Church to dominate personal and family life was soon extended to the duty of interference with secular government. Its maxim became *Cujus religio, ejus regio*, the converse of the mediaeval formula. Doubtless it is true, as has been argued, that the original aim, as shown by the use of the phrase the "crown honours of Christ," was less to aggrandise the Church than to exalt the majesty of our Lord. But in fact it was soon to develop into a claim which was inconsistent with any stable civil society.

Of this fatal heritage of the Middle Ages Knox was the chief exponent. The Reformation in Scotland was largely political, the work of laymen; its most effective champions, the nobles, owed their bitterness against Rome mainly to the desire to retain Church lands; so the relationship with the civil power was from the start a vital issue. Knox—*clarum et venerabile nomen*—one of the greatest destructive forces in our history and no mean constructive one, had immense shrewdness and practical wisdom, but he had little power of coherent thought. He is one of the most inconsistent of writers and speakers, and his mind is constantly in a passionate confusion. From such a man it was idle to expect any wise and cogent definition of the respective powers of State and Church. It was owing to him that the Reformation in Scotland went so deep ; but if he left his country the bequest of a noble democracy, he left it also a tradition of rigidity and intolerance and political strife.

For the essence of his conception of the Church was really that of unlimited authority. It could not choose but interfere in civil affairs. There was no agreement on what constituted an ecclesiastical offence ; an Edinburgh elder, for example, was ordered to do penance in the kirk for exporting wheat. Andrew Melville's famous declaration about the two kings and two kingdoms in Scotland might seem a reasonable statement of spiritual independence, but its occasion was a claim of the ministers to interfere in secular policy.[1] In theory, the Church professed to separate civil and ecclesiastical jurisdiction with scrupulous care, and it always objected to ecclesiastics holding civil offices ; but in fact no barrier could long stand, the Church's claims being what they were. The doctrine of the Headship of Christ was interpreted in the long run so as to overrule all lesser sanctions. That was the true root of the trouble over Episcopacy, and not a mere difference in the reading of certain New Testament passages. The Kings, James and Charles, desired a hierarchy so as to give them more control over the Church ; the Church desired the liberty of extending, when it so desired, its spiritual prerogatives into secular domains.

[1] Rait, *The Parliaments of Scotland*, 53.

Both based their arguments on divine right. It was a conflict of rival extremes.

III

Presbytery and Episcopacy

With high purpose and a sincere devotion, but with those perilous elements, which we have sketched, in its constitution, the Reformed Church of Scotland started upon its journey. It had come into being by its own act, independent of the civil power, for its birth was the General Assembly of 1560-61. At that date the national Church sprang into life ; seven years later an Act of Parliament made it an established Church ; that is to say, the State did not create the Church's authority, but recognised formally that which was already existing. Its organisation, its ritual, and even its doctrines were not yet wholly settled, but its spiritual autonomy was indisputable, since it owned no headship but Christ's.

It began in 1560 with a purely administrative Episcopacy, not possessed of orders higher than those of the ordinary ministry. The superintendents, or bishops, were subject to the control of the General Assembly, and the main purpose of their office was to perform the duties of local administration, which, under the influence of Andrew Melville, were, about 1580, assigned to the newly-instituted Church courts, known as presbyteries. The position, however, see-sawed according to the prestige of the King at the moment, for James did not admit the Church's claim of spiritual autonomy, and regarded an hierarchy as a necessary protection for the throne. In 1584 the Black Acts recognised the King as the head of the Church, and made the meetings of the General Assembly depend upon the permission of King and Parliament; in 1592 the position was reversed, and a complete Presbyterian polity was established; by 1600 James had triumphed again and bishops sat in Parliament. When he succeeded to the English throne he won a new authority, the Act of 1592 was repealed, and Episcopacy became the law. In the same way the Articles of Perth, ratified by Parliament in 1621, made customs approximate to the English rather than to the Genevan code, by enjoining kneeling at communion, confirmation, and the keeping of certain Church festivals.

But neither the parliamentary Episcopacy nor the Perth Articles greatly affected the life of the Church, for the law was not strictly enforced, and James had the wisdom to call a halt in his policy of religious uniformity. The discipline and practice were in substance Presbyterian, especially as regards local government. The General Assembly lost first its authority and then its existence, and the bishops exercised such political influence as remained to the Church. Their political power encouraged among their opponents that tendency by which the Church, under the inspiration of the Melvilles, came to regard itself more and more as a self-governing commonwealth, wholly independent in all things which by any stretch of language could be called spiritual. Knox had written : " The ordering and reformation of religion doth especially appertain to the Civil Magistrate. . . . The King taketh upon him to command the Priests." By 1620 no leader of Presbytery in Scotland but would have repudiated this dictum of its founder.

Yet in the first decades of the seventeenth century there was no final bar to uniformity between England and Scotland. The new impulse in religion had first come north of Tweed through the study of Wycliffe's Bible, and both nations had the Word of God in the same tongue. There was some justification for James's policy. Both Churches were Protestant and Calvinist ; both had liturgies which might have been made one had the advice of John Hales been followed, and a public form of service devised embracing only those things upon which all Christians were agreed.[1] There was an opportunity for a true eirenicon, as Archbishop Ussher believed, if bishops were required to follow the primitive practice and act on the advice of the ministers, laymen were brought into church management, and churchmen were disqualified for civil office. There was a real chance of union under James ; under Charles I. it vanished, and has not returned.

Episcopacy, in the attenuated form in which it had been now established, might well have been tolerated in spite of Andrew Melville's theoretic objections, since it bore so lightly on the ordinary man. It had not much prestige—the *tulchan* bishops had seen to that—but it roused no great antipathy, and it interfered little with Presbyterian usage. The trouble which began under Charles I. was due not to Episcopacy but

[1] See his *Tract concerning Schisme*, 1642.

to Prelacy. "Episcopacy," Sir Thomas Raleigh has written, "is a form of government, possessing a strong claim upon our respect and gratitude. Prelacy is a vice, and a vice which is not peculiar to the episcopal churches. It makes its appearance wherever a minister of the Word imagines that his office entitles him to exercise lordship over his brethren. It was in the Church from the first; for we remember how the companions of Christ disputed which of them should be greatest, and how Salome asked that her son should have the chief place in the Kingdom."[1] The prelate, as "one set above," was an offence to a Church which believed in the parity of ministers, and for the King to claim to alter ritual and interfere with Church government of his own will was to undermine the spiritual freedom which was the Church's chief foundation.

[1] *Annals of the Church in Scotland*, 10.

The Second Reformation

So we reach what is sometimes known as the Second Reformation, which was a revolt from Prelacy, as the First Reformation had been a revolt from Rome. Charles I. by his revocation of Church property in the hands of laymen had alarmed the nobles and barons, and thereby provided for the Church in her disputes a new set of Lords of the Congregation. He had established a court of High Commission, increased the number of bishops in the Privy Council to seven, and made Archbishop Spottiswoode Chancellor —the first time since the Reformation that the office had been given to a churchman. He passed from one blunder to another, driving even royalists like Drummond of Hawthornden into opposition, till in 1637 he imposed, by an act of pure autocracy, a new Prayer-book upon the Scottish Church. The result was to fire the heather and to unite all Scotland against him, except a few

Catholic nobles and Aberdeen doctors. The National Covenant was signed in the first months of 1638, a temperate and strictly legal assertion of the autonomy of the national Church. In November of the same year a General Assembly held at Glasgow, formally illegal, but with a solid nation behind it, decreed a root-and-branch abolition of Episcopacy and its ministrants.

It would have been well had the Church been content to stop there. With all the irregularities of its procedure, it had required that Scottish liberties should be safeguarded, and demanded in proof the grant of the kind of Church which the nation preferred. In its insistence upon spiritual freedom it had ample historical warrant. But the dangerous constituents in its heritage were now to come uppermost, and too many of its leaders had the vision of Hildebrand in their souls and the spirit of Hildebrand in their blood. It is a hazardous thing to claim that any system of church government is *divini juris*, unless it be granted that the claim can be shared among many systems. "Establish," said Coleman, preaching before the House of Commons in July 1645, "as few things by divine right as can well be." The claim to possess a monopoly of divine inspiration came from a casuistical and unscholarly interpretation of the Scriptures, and on the same basis Independent, Quaker, and Laudian Anglican could reach the same conclusion about his own belief. Of such, a premise uniformity was the logical consequence, and to insist upon it became a duty. This was the creed as much of Henderson and Guthrie as of Laud and Charles. "In the paradise of Nature," wrote Henderson in 1640, "the diversity of flowers and herbs is pleasant and useful, but in the paradise of the Church different and contrary religions are unpleasant and hurtful." Note that "different" and "contrary" were conjoined. Scotland claimed to dictate to England her ecclesiastical polity.

There was nobility in the dream, but it was a noble folly. The Scottish divines had never lost the vision of a single catholic and universal Church upon earth. You will find it in Melville and Brown of Wamphray; you will find it in Samuel Rutherford and James Durham, as well as in Archbishop Leighton. They never unchurched their old enemy Rome, or treated her baptism as invalid. They were always unwilling separatists, and longed for reunion—on their own terms. Durham is vehement against the divisions "occasioned by a carnal and factious-like pleading for and vindicating even of truth." They had a horror of light-hearted schism and a pathetic desire to see Christ's people in concord. Durham's congested style becomes on this subject almost eloquent:

"Never did men run to quench fire in a city, lest all should be destroyed, with more diligence than men ought to bestir themselves to quench this in the Church. Never did mariners use

> more speed to stop a leak in a ship, lest all should be drowned, than ministers especially and all Christian men should haste to stop this beginning of the breaking in of these waters of strife, lest thereby the whole Church be overwhelmed. And if the many evils which follow therefrom, the many commands whereby union is pressed, yea, the many entreaties and obtestations whereby the Holy Ghost doth so frequently urge this upon us all, as a thing most acceptable to Him and profitable to us—if, I say, these and many other considerations have not weight to convince of the necessity of this duty to prevent or heal a breach, we cannot tell what can prevail with men that profess reverence to the great and dreadful name of God, conscience of duty, and respect to the edification of the Church, and to their own peace at the appearance of the Lord in the great day, wherein the peacemakers shall be blessed, for they shall be called the children of God." [1]

But so long as there was no clear distinction between the essential and the inessential, so long as unity was identified with uniformity, this passionate desire for union became an

[1] *Treatise concerning Scandal* (1659), 313.

explosive to shatter instead of a cement to bind.

The result was the Solemn League and Covenant, signed in St. Margaret's Church, Westminster, in September 1643, and thereafter sworn to by the Estates and the General Assembly and the Scottish people, in which the Church violently encroached upon the sphere of secular government. It was regarded as a mystical covenant with the Almighty, its acceptance a test of faith, its rejection or breach a certain proof of damnation. This method of covenant-making was a lamentable descent into a legal formalism which degraded the whole conception of the relationship of God and His people. It had immediate and disastrous results. It set Scotland in sharp antagonism to a large part of the people of England ; it drove from the Scottish Church the greatest of its sons, Montrose ; it intensified the spirit of sectarian bigotry into which it was drifting ; it earned the hearty enmity of the foremost of

Englishmen, and of all those who, like Cromwell, were striving for toleration. But the labours of the divines at Westminster, the sponsors of the Solemn League, brought forth one worthy fruit. They produced an ordinal of public worship, and they codified their theology in the Confession of Faith, which has remained ever since in substance the doctrinal base of Scottish Presbytery.

The Restoration

The rule of Cromwell in Scotland meant the practical curbing of the theocracy into which the Church had drifted. The Restoration of 1660 meant the upturning of its foundations. The Church, having sought too much, was now to get less than its due, and that spiritual liberty which in its pride it had denied to others was now to be denied to itself. Just as the Glasgow Assembly of 1638 had abolished James's laws, so the Act Rescissory of 1661 blotted out twenty-three years of Presbyterian legislation. The restored Episcopacy resembled that of the reign of James rather than the Laudian ideal of uniformity with England. But it was the King who dictated the Church's constitution ; Episcopacy had become identified with the loss of liberty, and the issue was now not as to the merits or demerits of a form of government but as to whether the Church's autonomy was to be maintained. The Headship of Christ became the testing question. Most of Scotland, being very weary, settled down under the new regime, but in the south and west the flower of the ministers and laymen opposed the King. There was dross as well as fine gold in such men. The strife was largely one of rival intolerances, and the Covenanters held as firmly as Laud ever did to the principle of uniformity. They would have had all men compelled to adopt a single creed and practice, but that creed and practice must be their own. Yet they fought blindly and confusedly for one lasting truth, the Church's spiritual freedom, and, if only for their testimony on that behalf, they deserve to be held in honourable memory.

The Revolution of 1688 saw the close of the second great stage in the Church's history. That stage began with the Second Reformation when Prelacy was overthrown and the freedom of the Church was vindicated ; it ended with the Church in servitude to the civil authority, a lack-lustre nominal Episcopacy, and some of the best of the Scottish people outlaws for conscience sake. More serious still, the habit of separatism had grown, and the seamless robe of the Church was rent asunder. The quarrels of Resolutioner and Protester had been followed after the Restoration by the Covenanting breach, and the Covenanters themselves threatened to split up into lesser conventicles—" a poor, wasted, misrepresented Remnant," in the words of James Renwick's *Informatory Vindication*, " of the Suffering, Anti-Popish,

Anti-Prelatic, Anti-Erastian, Anti-Sectarian, true Presbyterian Church of Christ in Scotland."

Yet throughout that troubled age an ideal of a Church at peace with itself was never forgotten, and there is often more wisdom to be got from the writings of the divines than from their public utterances and actions. The ferment of the time produced many men of real, if one-sided, greatness. There were fervid evangelists who made a fire in cold places; scholars and thinkers like Robert Boyd and James Durham and Brown of Wamphray; mystics like Samuel Rutherford, whose saccharine sweetness often cloys, but who can rise now and then to an apocalyptic splendour; quaint souls like William Guthrie of Fenwick—a Scottish Traherne or Henry Vaughan—who bade his hearers praise God, "if ye have no more, for this good day and sunshine to the lambs"[1]; Leighton, a bishop of the Restora-

[1] Wodrow, *Analecta*, I. 137.

tion Episcopacy, whose sermons were Coleridge's delight, and who laboured for peace where peace could not be ; James Renwick, the last martyr, a man of wistful apostolic power. Most of them died young, worn out with an eternal dissidence, for they had to build God's house, like Nehemiah, with trowel in one hand and sword in the other. One and all they were men of a noble fortitude, confused sometimes and a little blind, but of a great stoutness of heart. In that age of suffering and darkness their eyes were always on the world beyond time, and often, in their too ardent contemplation of immortality, they were careless of mortal wisdom and the humbler mortal duties. Each " fired his ringing shot and passed " to the rest for which he was always longing. Their words were those of Cromwell—" We are indeed but a feeble and sickly company, yet we shall work the time that is appointed us, and after that rest in peace."

IV

The Revolution Settlement

The Revolution Settlement—mainly the work of William Carstares, who must rank high among ecclesiastical statesmen—was a peace of exhaustion. The fact that the Scottish bishops took the side of James made it certain that Episcopacy would disappear from the national Church. For the rest, Presbytery was established, patronage was abolished, and the Confession of Faith was made statute law. It seemed that the Church had been confirmed in its exclusive spiritual jurisdiction and its intrinsic spiritual powers. There was no mention of Covenants, or of the theocratic claims which had begun with the Glasgow Assembly of 1638; it was as if it had been tacitly agreed that that stormy chapter should be forgotten.

From this fatigued unanimity there were two main dissentients. Many of the Episcopalian clergy to their honour followed the King, whose divine right to the throne had been part of their creed. They paid the price of their loyalty, and the sufferings of those Scottish non-jurors are too often forgotten. There was justification for Pleydell's epithet for the communion to which he belonged—"the persecuted Episcopal Church of Scotland."[1] But in certain districts in the north, where that Church had a large popular following, the old regime continued undisturbed. It differed from that of Presbytery only in its acceptance of bishops, and in its attitude towards the reigning house. Its ritual was of the simplest, it celebrated communion according to the barest Presbyterian fashions, and its creed was indistinguishable from that laid down in the Confession of Faith.

The other dissentients were to be found in the south-west, the men of the Societies, who followed the blood-reddened banner of

[1] In *Guy Mannering*.

Richard Cameron and Donald Cargill. They claimed to be the historic Church of Scotland, compelled through the errors of the majority to withdraw themselves into private societies for Christian fellowship. For a decade or two they led a stormy life, lit by political intrigues; the Jacobites regarded them as likely allies, and their dealings with the Society men may be read in the unedifying pages of Ker of Kersland. The Cameronians held strictly to the Covenants, and could not acknowledge an uncovenanted Kirk or an uncovenanted King. By and by, through the work of men like John M'Millan of Balmaghie, the Societies were organised into a Presbytery, which ultimately became a Church—the Reformed Presbyterian Church of Scotland, the first and not the least estimable of Scottish secessions.

In 1712, by a mischievous trick of the English Tories and the Scottish Jacobites, patronage was restored, and the dragon's teeth were sown which were to produce a melancholy harvest. The Church protested against it, but for a little it was no great grievance, since ministers continued to be placed by the will of a congregation rather than by the nomination of a patron. But presently the patrons became more active, presbyteries refused to give assent to their wishes, and the General Assemblies were congested with appeals. The device of peripatetic "riding committees," sent abroad to settle disputes, was a solution which had no hope of permanence. Here was one rock of offence, the more dangerous because certain younger ecclesiastics, who were afterwards to be leaders of the Moderates, were anxious in this matter to make the Assembly dictate harshly to the presbyteries.

Another was the inclination to heresy hunts, a danger in all churches which have no strong spiritual inspiration. In 1695 Thomas Aikenhead, a lad of nineteen, who favoured a fantastic materialism and considered the Pentateuch to be post-Exilian, was tried and condemned. He recanted—which would have saved his life at the hands of the Inquisition—but was duly hanged in Edinburgh. Soon controversies arose in the inner circles of the orthodox. A century before, a certain fellow of Brasenose College, Oxford, had published a book called *The Marrow of Modern Divinity*, in which the doctrine of saving grace was stated in its extreme Calvinistic form. This ancient work was seized upon by those ministers who scented latitudinarian tendencies, and the " Marrow-men " became a dangerous left wing in the Church, trembling upon the brink of secession.

The Secessions

The result was an exemplification of that characteristic which Thomas Hobbes had long ago marked in Presbyterianism, a liability to hive off into sects. The first schism was that of the Erskines, who had been Marrow-men along with Boston of Ettrick; the ostensible ground was patronage and the growing Erastian character of the Church, though doctrinal dissatisfaction also played a part; they had never accepted the Revolution Settlement, and were still harking back upon the Covenants like the old Protesters.[1] "There is a difference to be made," wrote Ebenezer Erskine, "between the Established Church of Scotland and the Church of Christ in Scotland"; and he proceeded to constitute the latter as a secession Church. That was in 1733, and twelve years later there was a secession within this secession. It turned on the validity of the burgess oath—whether one could conscientiously swear to uphold "the true religion presently professed within this realm." Those who maintained that the

[1] Cf. Lord Sands' paper in *Records of the Scottish Church History Society*, 1928.

establishment was corrupt could scarcely approve such a form of words. So the first secession split into Burgher and Anti-Burgher, and half a century later the former split again into New Lights and Old Lights, according to the degree of modernism among its members. The same division showed itself among the Anti-Burghers, the eternal dichotomy of conservatives and progressives. The basis was partly doctrinal, but far more that old rock of Scottish controversy, the relation of Church and State.

There was still a third hiving-off in 1761, in the Relief Church, whose founder was Thomas Gillespie, and which had a more liberal character than its predecessors. The brethren of the Relief had no enthusiasm for the letter of the Covenants. "I do not think," wrote Patrick Hutchison, "that ever any part of the Church of Christ, since the commencement of the Christian era, was more deeply involved in the guilt of ignorant and false swearing than the British subjects in the last century." [1] They held, too, by comprehensive communion, for their synod in 1773 declared: "It is agreeable to the Word of God and their principles occasionally to hold communion with those of the Episcopal and Independent persuasions who are visible saints."

Moderatism

The various secessions profoundly weakened the Church of Scotland by withdrawing from it many men of true religious genius. The ranks of the establishment closed up in a dry and formal unity against a menace which was real enough, for by 1766 there were 120 secession meeting-houses attended by more than 100,000 worshippers. The consequence was the Moderatism which for more than a century was the dominant policy of the Church. The Moderates had many

[1] *Compendious View of the Religious System of the Synod of Relief*, 1779.

merits, and it is as unfair to judge them by a pagan like "Jupiter" Carlyle, as it would be to judge their opponents, the High-flyers, by Dr. Webster of the Tolbooth Church, the "Dr. Magnum Bonum" of many tales, who had the bad taste to complain that while he drank with gentlemen he must vote with fools. A man like William Robertson, the historian and Principal of Edinburgh University, was as orthodox in theology as any seceder, and far more liberal and tolerant. The party did a useful work in lowering the temperature in ecclesiastical controversy, and loosening the bonds of antiquarian dogmas.

But none the less they were a chilling influence in Scotland. The piety of their devout men—and they had many—was apt to be without fervour, and so without popular appeal. Their clergy were aloof from their parishioners, and inclined, under the blight of patronage, to be subservient to the local gentry. They had their own intolerances. If they were free on the whole from what Melancthon called the *rabies theologorum*, they had a stiff legalism not less distasteful. They were hostile to all missionary and evangelical effort, and Chalmers' summary was not untrue of the majority:

> " A morality without godliness, a certain prettiness of sentiment served up in tasteful and well-turned periods of composition—the ethics of philosophy or of the academic chair rather than the ethics of the Gospel, the speculations of natural theology, or, perhaps, an ingenious and scholarlike exposition of the credentials, rather than a faithful exposition of the contents of the New Testament ; these, for a time, dispossessed the topics of other days, and occupied that room in our pulpits which had formerly been given to the demonstration of sin and the Saviour."

A religion without enthusiasm is a religion without life and without hope of growth. Also, this enlightenment had its childish side. The ministers who thronged to the performance of Home's *Douglas*, and flocked after

Mrs. Siddons, and made a parade of their little liberties, have to me an indescribable air of naughty urchins.

But Moderatism, great as were its defects, made its own contribution to the development of Church and nation. It meant the abandonment for good and all of the fantastic theocratic dreams of the previous century. It was a disintegrating force when brought to bear on certain debasing superstitions. The Church, for all the dialectical power of its theology, had been slow to apply the same vigour of mind to the examination of witchcraft and cognate beliefs, and as late as 1697 we have the amazing case of Christian Shaw of Bargarran, who was tormented by devils, a story which carries us back to the heart of the Middle Ages. Good men like Wodrow and bad men like Lord Grange were alike opposed to a relaxation of the savage witchcraft laws. But, as the eighteenth century advanced, the light of common-sense began to penetrate the darkness, and we find Mr. Fraser of Tiree and Mr. Campbell of Aberfeldy treating "Satan's invisible world" as a subject for cool scientific inquiry. Hutcheson's lectures on moral philosophy at Glasgow prepared the way for that *Aufklärung* which, however shallow its inspiration, was at any rate the foe of the blinder superstitions.

Let it not be forgotten that it is to the Moderates that we owe an infusion of the rationalistic spirit, "sapping a solemn creed with solemn sneer," which is an ingredient in all progress. It was the only path to toleration, since, as Charles James Fox once said, for toleration there is needed a certain degree of honest scepticism. Behind all their cant and foppery there was this solid achievement—the provision of the necessary sceptical dissolvent for belated or perverse dogmas. They preached the forgotten lesson of the importance of the human reason in all human endeavour, and they strove to link religion to those other spheres of intellectual effort from which it had too long been divorced. Without the help of this uninspired and matter-of-fact sagacity Scotland would have been slow to clear her feet of mediaeval lumber. Theirs was the same spirit which in the secular world made her turn her back upon vain dreams of separation and revolt and work out for herself her economic salvation.

It is a mistake, I think, to regard the ecclesiastical life of the capital city in the eighteenth century as truly reflecting the religious life of Scotland. The ministers satirised by Burns had no doubt their counterparts in most shires, "cauld harangues" were varied by the "Gospel club," and the hungry sheep were fed now with a drab morality, now with superheated imaginings, and now with barren scholastic subtleties. But the records of kirk sessions and presbyteries show us that the plain evangel was widely taught by wise and simple preachers. Survivals of the old, stern tradition of the saints kept the spiritual fires alight, even within the Church, and most Lowland parishes could boast a David Deans or a Gifted Gilfillan. The central Borders had shared less than many districts in the Covenanting fervours, but we may read in James Hogg how real a thing religion was in the life of the Border peasant. He made the Bible the lamp of his path, and at family prayers communed fearlessly with his Maker. " The flocks on a thousand hills are Thine and their lives and death wad be naething to Thee. Thou wad naither be the richer nor the poorer, but, oh Lord, it 's a great matter to huz." Nor was the spirit of critical independence absent, and he was under no blind bondage to the letter of the Word. The householder would stop his reading of the Bible with the remark : " If it hadna been the Lord's will, that verse had been better left out." We have already travelled far from Samuel Rutherford.

The End of the Century

With the end of the eighteenth century came the dawning of a new world. The *Aufklärung* gave place, in literature, to the Romantic Revival. Robert Burns interpreted Scotsmen to one another and wove into one poetic tradition the conflicting strains in our history. Sir Walter Scott revealed his country to itself and to the world. Scotland had set her house in order, her industries were entering upon an era of wide expansion, and her agriculture was rapidly becoming a model to all Britain. Political thought, stimulated by the French Revolution, was no longer content with a museum piece like the Scottish system of representation, and doctrines were professed by reputable citizens which would have sent their fathers to the gallows. Of this stirring in men's minds there were two main consequences. Scotland's nationalism was intensified, and her pride enlarged ; she was resolved to hold by her past as well as to march boldly towards the future. Again, the critical spirit was abroad, and it was certain that no doctrine or institution would be long exempt from it.

The century closed with an established Church in uneasy alliance with the State, and a number of secession churches, free indeed from such entanglements, but shackled with heavy dogmatic bonds. Some of the old matters of dispute had been shed. Prelacy would never again interfere with Presbytery, and the removal of its disabilities in 1792 enabled the Scottish Episcopal Church to follow its own natural development. The Covenants were no longer a dead hand, even in the sects which had left the parent Church because of them. There was a movement towards a more liberal construction of the Creed, and wise men were beginning to hold the true Reformation view—that a living Church must be free to change its confessions within the wide limits of the Scripture faith. In the Church of Scotland itself the State establishment was a cardinal principle, but it had lost the dangerous rider which the seventeenth century had given it ; if it still based itself on the text in Isaiah, "Kings shall be thy nursing fathers and queens thy nursing mothers," it did not press the second clause of the verse, "They shall bow down to thee with their faces towards the earth and lick up the dust of thy feet." Indeed, the Church's pretensions as regards the State had become humility itself, and patronage tended to make it a disconsidered dependent.

Yet in the minds of many there was a vision of a national religion, "the restoration," in Montrose's words, "of that which our first Reformers had." Among the seceders there was little valuing of secession for its own sake, and some of their leaders were beginning to dream of an eventual unity. And in all the various kirks there was growing up a conception of what

Presbytery might yet become, a faith of which Principal Rainy, in his reply to Dean Stanley, has given a classic definition :

> " Presbyterianism meant organised life, regulated distribution of forces, graduated recognition of gifts, freedom to discuss, authority to control, agency to administer. Presbyterianism meant a system by which the convictions and conscience of the Church could constantly be applied, by appropriate organs, to her current affairs. Presbyterianism meant a system by which quickening influence, experienced anywhere in the Church, could be turned into effective form and transmitted to fortify the whole society. Presbyterianism meant a system by which any one, first of all the common man, had his recognised place, his defined position, his ascertained and guarded privileges, his responsibilities inculcated and enforced, felt himself a part of the great unity, with a right to care for its welfare and to guard its integrity. From the broad base of the believing people, the sap rose through Sessions, Presbyteries, Synods, to the Assembly, and, thence descending, diffused knowledge, influence, unanimity through the whole system.

Presbyterianism is a system for a free people that love a regulated, a self-regulating freedom."

It was a great ideal, which still awaits its full accomplishment.

V

The Opening Salvos

The nineteenth century was to see at once a movement towards union and a further disruption, for much had to be pulled down before a new and ampler building could arise. Scotland, for the better part of a hundred years, was filled with controversy, which, if less bitter and more fruitful than that of the seventeenth century, was scarcely less vehement and continuous. To the detached observer it seemed that the land was spending its strength in barren debate. In an " Appeal to the Clergy of the Church of Scotland," published in 1875, Robert Louis Stevenson wrote :—" It would be difficult to exaggerate the pity that fills my heart at such a reflection ; at the thought of how this neck of barren hills between two inclement seaways has echoed for three centuries with the uproar of sectarian battles ; of how the east wind has carried out the sound of our shrill disputation into the desolate Atlantic, and the west wind has borne it over the German Ocean, as though it would make all Europe privy to how well we Scottish brethren abide together in unity. It is not a bright page in the annals of a small country." Yet it is hard to see how this epoch of controversy could have been avoided, though it might well have been curtailed. There were in dispute matters of moment which were capable of no easy solution, but for which a solution must be found if the Church in Scotland was to fulfil its mission.

During the first decades of the century there were stirrings of life in many quarters. Men like Erskine of Linlathen and M'Leod

Campbell were feeling their way towards a more liberal theology. An evangelical movement, which may be said to represent in Scotland the ultimate ripples of the great tidal wave of Wesley's work in England, was putting life into the dry bones of orthodoxy. In the Highlands especially, the "Men," prophets of an antique stamp, brought to the preaching of the Gospel the passion and mysticism of the Celt. In the secession Churches scholars were arising, like Robertson of Irvine and John Cairns, who illuminated Scottish divinity with a scholarship drawn from France and Germany. Missionary enterprise was beginning—in India under Alexander Duff, in South Africa under David Livingstone and Robert Moffat.

But, for the rest, the rule of the past was strictly obeyed. Church architecture retained its pristine hideousness. A Scottish service followed the meagre Puritan fashion—not that of the first Reformers—and was in the main a lengthy monologue by the preacher. Patronage lay heavy on the Church, and the dominant Moderate party were stiff legalists both in doctrine and practice. In dogma they held by the letter of the Westminster Confession; in ecclesiastical policy they inclined to emphasise the dependence of the Church upon the civil law. Their conservatism was less a political creed than a temperamental bias, for they held, like Lady Rachel Drummond, that "a new light could enter only through a crack either in the head or in the heart." They were, in Lord Cockburn's phrase, that inexorable type of revolutionary "which will change nothing voluntarily, and thus compels everything to change itself forcibly."

As the century advanced the new forces gathered strength, and it was very clear that ere long there must be conflict. The new wine was too strong for the old bottles. The example of the secession Churches made it certain that the issue would be joined upon patronage. The majority of the reform party were on the progressive side in politics, but their leader, Thomas Chalmers, was a staunch Conservative, who professed a "moral loathing" for the Whigs. In the Assembly of 1832, under his Moderatorship, the question was raised of a popular veto upon the nomination of a patron. One suggestion was that the Legislature should be petitioned to abolish patronage, a course which might well have succeeded ; but the predominant view was that the Church itself should legislate on the matter. The consequence was the passing in 1834 of a Veto Act, which laid down that a majority of the male heads of households, being communicants, were empowered to veto a presentation. At the same time the question was raised of the new chapels of ease, supported by voluntary effort, which were springing up in populous parts of the country, and the ministers of which, not being parish ministers, could not sit in Church courts. The Chapel Act, passed in the same year, put such ministers on an equality with the rest, and thereby greatly increased the anti-Moderate element in future Assemblies.

The Ten Years' Conflict

Thus began what is known as the "Ten Years' Conflict," in which the whole relations of Church and State were brought into controversy. The matter at issue was not the legality of patronage, which was admitted, but the right of the Church to control its procedure. The exponents both of the new evangelicalism and of the new democracy protested against the notion of a unitary state with complete jurisdiction over all departments of life. The old war-cry of the "Headship of Christ" was heard again, and there were wild words spoken; the extremists, like the Covenanters, were often deficient in reverence and humour; the right to veto a presentee was described as a right "purchased by the Redeemer with His blood" ; and there were evangelical leaders who seemed to advocate a new papalism. But behind the extravagance a great and historic principle was at stake, the self-governing powers of the Church. The pity was that the policy adopted in the Veto and Chapel Acts kept the quarrel inside the narrow domain of law. The difficulty lay in the confounding of two different words, "jurisdiction" and "authority." The Church could claim authority derived from its divine founder, but when it claimed for its courts "exclusive jurisdiction," the right to declare and enforce law, it entered the perilous pale of legal subtleties. A problem, which should have been solved by statesmen, was unhappily left to the lawyers.

A crop of lawsuits, the Auchterarder case, the Lethendy case, the Marnoch or Strathbogie case, showed that the Scottish tribunals were adverse to the Church's claim, and the

House of Lords affirmed their judgment. Then, too late, recourse was had to the Government. But neither Melbourne nor his successor Peel was sympathetic. It was impossible to make an English statesman understand the true inwardness of a problem with such an idiomatically Scottish background. Moreover, there were two special difficulties. The evangelical party in the Scottish Church was a High Church party, making a bold claim for religious independence; the same claim was being urged by the Oxford Tractarians, who were associated with a revolt against Protestantism, as most men understood it. The Cabinet was staunchly Protestant, and undoubtedly in their eyes the Scottish case was fatally prejudiced by its points of resemblance with the Oxford Movement. Again, the claim of the Church, with its insistence upon "exclusive jurisdiction," seemed to many inconsistent with the whole genius of the common law. As Lord Cockburn put it :

"A claim of jurisdiction by the Church, though only to spiritual effects, altogether exclusive of civil control, is so repugnant to modern British notions, that, after the Court decided it to be ill-founded, it is not wonderful that any Government should recoil from attempting to legalise it, even if it could be supposed that any Parliament could have been got to sanction such a measure. . . . It is plain to me that the Church of Scotland had the jurisdiction, and that its practical exercise, as proved by immemorial experience, was quite safe. But, the decision being otherwise, I do not see how any Government, relishing the decision, could do anything but adopt the law delivered by the Court. Its error lay in relishing it." [1]

The Disruption and its Prize

For the reform party there could be no going back. In 1842, at the "last Assembly of the united Church of Scotland," a resolution condemning patronage was moved by William Cunningham, supported by

[1] *Journal*, ii. 35.

Chalmers, and carried by a large majority. That Assembly also adopted what became famous as the "Claim of Right," which laid down as the basis of the national Church the sole Headship of Christ, and the government of the Church in the hands of office-bearers distinct from the civil magistrates. The Cabinet received these declarations with apathy and refused to act. Disruption was now probable; the defeat in March 1843 of Mr. Fox Maule's motion to appoint a committee to inquire into the whole question made it certain.[1] On the 18th of May the Assembly met in St. Andrew's Church in Edinburgh, a dramatic scene which has been often described. The Moderator, Dr. David Welsh, read a solemn protest, and then moved to the door, followed by Chalmers and Candlish and Cunningham

[1] The Scottish members voted for the motion in a proportion of two to one, and the defeat was due to English votes. History repeated itself two years ago when the Revised Prayer-book was rejected by Scottish and Irish votes.

and a host of ministers and elders. Through an alley in a vast multitude they marched down the slopes which look upon the Firth to Tanfield Hall in Canonmills, where Chalmers was chosen Moderator by acclamation, and, after the singing of "Durie's Psalm,"[1] the first Assembly was constituted of the Free Church of Scotland.

To Gladstone, the High Churchman, the Disruption seemed a "noble and heart-stirring spectacle." "Away," he cried, "with the senile doctrine that religion cannot live but by the aid of parliaments!" The cool sagacity of Lord Cockburn pronounced it "the most honourable fact for Scotland that its whole history supplies." Such praise was amply deserved. That four hundred and seventy-four ministers should surrender a certain livelihood for a matter of conscience was a vindication of the essential nobility of human nature. Moreover, this matter of conscience

[1] The 124th in the second Scottish metrical version.

was no mere pedantry, but a profound principle of Scottish religious life. But of the majority who remained behind not all were over-careful of the " loaves and fishes," not all were formalists and reactionaries and obscurantists. There were young men like Norman Macleod, who were afraid—and not without reason—of a new high-flying Presbyterian priestcraft, for a kind of sacerdotalism has always been a peril in the Scottish Church. And many, whose sympathies were with those who broke away, were restrained by the honest belief that the true way of reform does not lie through separation, that a schism once it has taken place is hard to bridge, and that by preserving the historic continuity of an institution there is a hope of its reconstruction which departs if it be split asunder. To such, as to the loyalists in the American Revolution, history has been perhaps somewhat less than just.

The new Free Church must remain to all

time a model of bold and provident organisation. This greatest of Scottish secessions was a masterpiece of constructive genius. From the start it undertook all the duties of a national communion. In its first year it built five hundred churches ; it founded and carried on schools and religious ordinances in every part of the land ; it established its own colleges, and it supported its own ministry. It collected money at the rate of a thousand pounds a day, and thereby taught Scotsmen a new conception of liberality. Since every overseas missionary but one had joined it, it carried on its shoulders the whole missionary burden of the Church it had left. It had as its leaders the ablest theologians and the most popular preachers in Scotland, and it had among its rank and file the flower of her youth. In such a situation it was small wonder that the new Church carried its head high and was not altogether free from spiritual and intellectual pride. Lord Cockburn thought that the splendour of their new position had cured all the old defects of the anti-Moderates—“ except,” he adds dryly, “ fanaticism, which it will probably increase.”

“ We quit,” said Chalmers in a famous passage, “ a vitiated Establishment, but would rejoice in returning to a pure one. To express it otherwise, we are the advocates for a national recognition, and a national support of religion, and we are not voluntaries.” But though the great majority shared Chalmers’s view on this point, it is clear that it was not an obligatory article of belief. Soon after the Disruption the Free Church had to devise a formula which should embody its binding principle, and in that formula establishment was not included. The binding principle was “ the freedom and spirituality of the Church of Christ and her subjection to Him as her only Head, and His Word as her only standard.” The form which Chalmers’s doctrine came presently to take was a belief in a national recognition of religion, an insistence upon the general duty of nations and their rulers to protect the welfare of the Church and the interests of Christianity. It may be best expressed, perhaps, in Cromwell's words: "If any whosoever think the interests of Christians and the interests of the nation inconsistent or two different things, I wish my soul may never enter into their secret." The Free Church did not repudiate an establishment, provided it was combined with complete spiritual independence, but its cardinal principle was the second, and it soon inclined to grow apathetic about the first. It claimed to be the continuing Church of Scotland, the direct heir of the Reformation, the true repository of the traditions of Knox and Melville and Henderson, and such credentials were not made more splendid by any nod of assent from the State.

The Abolition of Patronage

Chalmers died and new men appeared, men without his conservatism and deep historic sense, and sometimes without his charity. The new Church advanced from strength to strength, its missionary enterprise brought it the admiration of the world, and soon its scholarship was not less famous than its evangelical zeal. It would have been strange if in such circumstances it had not developed a certain proud exclusiveness. Not all his successors could have said truly with Chalmers, "Who cares about the Free Church compared with the Christian good of the people of Scotland? . . . Be assured that the moral and religious well-being of the population is of infinitely higher importance than the advancement of any sect." Toleration was not a common mood. Its battles, internal and external, were stubbornly and bitterly fought.

Meantime the Church of Scotland, dazed

for some years by the shock of the Disruption, was slowly putting its house in order. Younger men were arising in its ranks —Norman Macleod, Tulloch and Caird, Charteris and Flint and Story, who had none of the old Moderate obscurantism, and who as preachers, thinkers and ecclesiastical statesmen could compare with the best in any communion. The first duties were to get rid of compromising lumber and to awaken the Church to its proper task. Robertson of Ellon carried out a large scheme of Church extension and endowment, and the duties of education, and of home and foreign missions, were undertaken in a new spirit. In 1852 ecclesiastical tests were abolished in the universities except for theological chairs, and finally, in 1874, after many futile attempts, patronage disappeared.

No doubt there were blunders in tactics. Considering all that had gone before, it would have been well if the Church of Scotland had taken the Free Church into its confidence and carried it with it in the various stages for the abolition of what had been the original rock of stumbling. Many churchmen believed — Norman Macleod among them—that the disappearance of patronage would open the road to re-union. But the Free Church had travelled far since 1843. Towards the removal of the handicaps of the sister Church it showed itself either apathetic or hostile, so that Mr. Arthur Balfour was compelled to ask in the House of Commons whether one religious sect could have a vested interest in the abuses of another. It held, not unnaturally, that what had driven it into the wilderness should not be removed without some confession of past error, or even restitution. It feared that the now liberated Church of Scotland might draw to itself seceders from its ranks who had forgotten, or had never understood, that patronage was the occasion rather than the cause of the breach of 1843.

An inevitable outcome was a demand for disestablishment. Resolutions in its favour were carried by large majorities in the Free Church Assembly and the United Presbyterian Synod in 1874. During the next six years the agitation grew, and with the return of Mr. Gladstone to power in 1880 it became a matter of party politics. The Liberal Prime Minister was never more than half-hearted on the question, and the emergence of Irish Home Rule as the main topic of political controversy, and the consequent schism in the Liberal party, put it beyond the sphere of the practicable.

The best of the Free Church leaders advocated disestablishment because they believed that it was the only basis for an ultimate Presbyterian unity in Scotland. But others—as was shown by the opposition to the Bill introduced by Mr. Finlay (afterwards Lord Chancellor of England) to declare the exclusive right of the Church of Scotland to regulate all matters spiritual by its own courts "not subject to interdict, reduction, suspension or any matter of review by any court of civil jurisdiction"—were influenced by the less worthy fear of losing, through the abolition of patronage, members to the other Church. To the historian it may well appear that for one communion to enlist the help of a political party, temporarily in power, in order to enforce something which another communion vehemently dislikes was the extreme of Erastianism, if that word have any meaning. It was fortunate that the movement failed, but it may be that the raising of the question had its own value, for it beaconed one perilous path, and prevented the minds of those who followed after unity from straying into fruitless fields.

During those years influences were at work in Scotland to broaden the dogmatic basis of faith and to enrich the traditional worship. There were many who in cult desired to return to the way of the first Reformers and to get rid of the alien Puritan belief that ugliness was indispensable for godliness. In matters of creed the Free Church was the pioneer. The tragic issue of the Robertson Smith case did more to liberalise its theology than if the great heresiarch had remained in its fold. It burst for good and all the bonds of a blind Scripture literalism, and his historical standpoint, in no way inconsistent with faith, became the creed of all thinking men. " In the Bible alone I find God drawing near to man in Christ Jesus and declaring to us in Him His Will for our salvation, and this record I know to be true by the witness of His Spirit in my heart, whereby I am assured that none other than God Himself is able to speak such words to my soul." In the Church of Scotland, too, men like John Caird were linking religion with an idealist conception of the world, and insisting that spiritual truths stood in need of constant re-statement, since creeds and theories are transient things, and no single one can be taken as the final and infallible interpretation of God's mind to man. The Church in Scotland, under the challenge of a new environment, was following the inexorable biological law and modifying its structure.

Reform and Rebuff

Meantime, among the non-established Churches, there had been during the century a steady drawing together. The wise course was followed whereby those closest to each other united, and thereby formed a potent centre to attract further adhesions. In 1847, the year of Chalmers' death, in Tanfield Hall, the scene of the Disruption, a new Church was born—the United Presbyterian, formed by the union of the Secession and Relief bodies—a Church at once orthodox and liberal, which was destined to play a great part in the religious life of Scotland. In 1852 the majority of the Original Seceders were received into the Free Church, and in

1876 the majority of the Reformed Presbyterians. Just as in the Free Church some form of establishment was generally accepted as desirable, but was not made a cardinal principle, so among the United Presbyterians what was known as "voluntaryism," while not an obligatory tenet, was the view of the majority.

Voluntaryism meant an aversion not only to State control, but to any kind of State connection. It was not the extreme atomism of Independency, for it contemplated an organised Church. On the negative side it was inclined to the view that a civil government had no concern with religion; on the positive side it laid down the duty of congregations to support the preaching of the Word by free-will gifts. This positive side alone was included in the standards of the Church; the negative side was left to the taste of individual members. It may fairly be said that the United Presbyterian Church had not in its articles any renunciation of an establishment, so long as spiritual autonomy and religious equality were safeguarded, or even of endowment, provided the duty of voluntary giving was not forgotten. And in men like John Cairns there was a burning vision of religious peace in Scotland—nay, more, of

> "a Church which, while separately organised in different countries, shall be one in basis and spirit, taking the Reformed Faith as its creed, simplicity as its guide in worship, and the Bible as its supreme standard, but which both in formation and administration must be independent and free from control by civil powers." [1]

Clearly no barrier of doctrine or practice stood between the Free Church and the United Presbyterian Church if establishment was not a cardinal tenet of the one or voluntaryism of the other. But this natural union was long delayed. From 1863 onward there was a second Ten Years' Conflict

[1] MacEwen, *Life of Cairns*, 301.

within the Free Church on the matter, but the efforts of the majority were thwarted by the "Constitutional" party under Begg, and they relinquished their campaign in fear of a threatened schism. "Disruption pride' was still too strong a thing. A tribute is due from the chronicler to the dignity and wisdom of the United Presbyterian leaders during this difficult time.

The movement was resumed in 1896, by which date both Churches had by means of declaratory acts broadened the basis of their articles of faith. This is not the place to tell the tale of the different stages in the advance to union, in which Dr. Rainy was the leader, as he had been the colleague of Candlish and Buchanan in the abortive attempt a quarter of a century before. By 1900 all difficulties had been surmounted, and on the 30th day of October of that year the Union was formally consummated. The achievement formed a happy precedent, for in the new United Free Church neither of the constituent bodies surrendered anything: things on which they had formerly differed remained open questions; it was union without uniformity; the points of contact were the fundamentals.

The Church Case

A section of the more conservative party in the Free Church, mostly living in the Highlands, refused to enter the Union, and constituted themselves the Free Church of Scotland. What followed will be long remembered. They brought an action at law to have themselves declared the historic Free Church and therefore the owners of the Church's property, which was held on trust for the principles of that Church's constitution—principles, they alleged, violated by the Union. They were unsuccessful in the Scottish courts, but in August 1904 the House of Lords on appeal, by a majority of three, gave judgment in their favour. It is probable that future ages will regard the verdict as at least dubious, and look to the dissenting judgments, like Lord Lindley's, for sounder law and sounder history.

But the supreme court of the land had decided, and its judgment must be accepted. Dr. Rainy, now within sight of eighty, faced the crisis in the spirit of Chalmers, and in his third Moderatorship steered his Church through the storm. Money was collected for immediate needs, as in the days of the Disruption ; there were few words spoken of bitterness or complaint ; the help of the State was called in to redress an impossible situation : a Royal Commission divided the property in accordance with the needs and capacities of the two parties, and an Act of Parliament made this apportionment law. A clause in that Act gave the Church of Scotland the right to revise its formula of subscription on the lines of the declaratory acts of the other Churches. In the General Assembly of 1905 the United Free Church in a solemn declaration reasserted its claim to spiritual liberty, on lines similar to the resolution of the Assembly in 1838.

The judgment of the House of Lords was the proximate cause of Scottish Church Union. Already the main obstacles had gone. The Covenants, with all their dangerous implications, were now things of only antiquarian interest. The Churches had long withdrawn themselves inside their spiritual domain and abandoned all theocratic pretensions. The antique literalism with which the Bible had been interpreted was discarded, and their theology had been at once broadened and vivified. Patronage with all its ugly concomitants had disappeared. Spiritual liberty, which involved liberty to change within certain limits, had become everywhere an accepted article of faith. There was a juster distinction made between fundamentals and "circumstantials," between essential tenets and open questions; and unity was conceived of as possible without a drab uniformity. This general consensus had come about in the right way, since old dogmas had not been formally renounced but had faded out of the intellectual air. A thousand matters of ancient dispute had become simply meaningless. Toleration, moreover, so far from being regarded as a soul-killing vice, was seen to be in itself a religious duty.

The events of August 1904 completed this clearing of the ground. As far back as 1767 Lord Mansfield had laid it down that voluntary Churches were "established," since, being tolerated, they had a place of security in the commonwealth.[1] The word was ceasing to have the sinister connotation which it had possessed since the Disruption. It was now clear that from a certain kind of establishment no Church could be free, since, if it owned property, it was bound by the terms of endowment, and, if it sought to change, might find itself compelled to

[1] *Corporation of London* v. *Evans* (H. of L.), Holliday, 225.

choose between impoverishment and liberty. Declarations of independence were not enough; it must secure the State's co-operation in safeguarding such independence. The State had restored to the United Free Church the patrimony which it had lost through a lesser union; it might well be asked to assist in opening the way to a greater.

*A Poetic Outcry**

From Alexander Cargill, Elder of the Kirk of the Remnant in the Vale of Wae, to the Reverend Murdo Mucklethraw, Minister of the Aforesaid Kirk, anent the great case recently argued in the House of Lords.

* The Epistle below was sent to 'Maga' by the recipient, the Reverend Mr. Mucklethraw, early in July, but as the case was still *sub judice* it was considered wise to postpone Mr. Cargill's "intelligent anticipation" until the Lords had delivered judgment.—Ed. 'Maga.' This piece was first published in *Blackwood's Edinburgh Magazine,* No. MLXVII, September 1904, Vol. CLXXVI, pp. 297–302. We reprint it here by kind permission of Messrs Blackwood, Pillans & Wilson Ltd. of Edinburgh.

Dear Reverend Sir,—I tak my pen
To tell yon great occasion when
We gart our licht shine afore men,
Yea, far and wide,
And smote the oppressor but and ben
For a' his pride.

Yoursel', ye mind, was far frae weel—
A cauld ye catch't at Kippenshiel,
Forbye rheumatics in your heel—
And thus it came,
Fou though ye were o' holy zeal,
Ye stopped at hame.

For me, my lambin'-time was bye,
The muirland hay was nane sae high,
The men were thrang, the grund was dry,
Sae when ye spak,
And bade me gang and testify,
I heldna back.

Wi' dowie hert I left that morn,
Reflectin' on the waefu' scorn
The Kirk maun thole, her courts forlorn,
Her pillars broke,
While Amalek exalts his horn,
And fills his poke.

I pondered the mischances sair
The Lord had gart puir Scotland bear
Frae English folk baith late and ear'
    Sin' Flodden year
To the twae beasts at Carlisle fair
    I bocht ower dear.

If true religion got a fa'
Frae her auld courts and guid Scots law,
What hope o' succour far awa'
    'Mang godless chiels,
Whae at the Word sae crousely craw
    And fling their heels.

As weel expect the Gospel sap 'ill
Rise in uncovenantit thrapple
As saw a ploom to raise an aipple,
    Or think a soo
Fleein' aloft on the hoose-tap 'ill
    Sit like a doo.

I like an owl in desert was,
When to the coorts I buid to pass,
Amang the crood to hear the Cause.
    Nae freend I saw,—
Just some auld men set oot in raws
    And belchin' law

But ane sat cockit in atween,
A wee man but as gleg's a preen:
A walth o' sense was in his een
    And foreheid massy.
"The Chancellor," I was tellt, when keen
    I speired whae was he.

Wi' prayerfu' mind I watched the stert
While Maister Johnston played his pairt,
And sune I fand my anxious hert
    Gie a great loup.
"Yon Chancellor the ungodly's cairt,"
    I said, "will coup."

O sir, that day I kent indeed
There's men o' worth across the Tweed,
Men whae are steadfast in the creed
    As Moses sel',
Men whae the Word o' God can read
    And cling to Hell.

I thocht they were a careless race,
Dozened wi' heathen commonplace,
Whae traivelled a' in slippery ways,
    Whase thochts were vain:
But noo I ken they've gifts and grace
    E'en like my ain.

A Lowden chiel—black be his tryst!—
A wise-like man, but ill advised,
Led on the hosts o' Antichrist,
    And threepit bauld,
That man could never back be wysed
    To Calvin's fauld.

He made the yett o' Heaven sae wide
The veriest stirk could get inside:
Puffed up he was wi' warldly pride
    And fou o' German,
Quotin' auld pagans for his guide
    And sic-like vermin.

He feucht wi' Prophets, jouked wi' Psalms,
He got his legs clean ower the trams,
He gart th' Apostles skip like rams
    To dae his biddin's:
Oor auld Confessions were but shams,
    Their loss guid riddance.

"God foreordained some men to Hell"—
Granted, but man can please himsel'
Up to a point—and if I dwell
    Mair on free-will
Than on election, I do well,
    A Christian still.

"For these are mysteries," quo' he,
"Whereon nae twae men can agree,
And sae it's richt for you and me—
    The thing's sae kittle—
Ane to consider half a lee,—
    Whilk maitters little.

"It's a'," he said, "confüsion wild;
In siccan things the best's a child;
Some walk an ell and some a mile;
    But dinna fear,
Thae doots will a' be reconciled
    In higher sphere.

"Therefore a kirk, whase lamps are bright,
Bequeathed by auld divines o' might,
Can fling them tapsalteerie quite,
    And think nae shame;
For white is black and black is white,
    It's a' the same."

But what availed his carnal lear
Against a man o' faith and prayer?
As through the thristles gangs the share
    And dings them doun,
E'en sae the Chancellor cleft him fair
    Frae heel to croun.

He pinned him wi' the Bible words,
He clove at him wi' Calvin's swirds,
He gart him loup aboot the boards
  Wi' muckle mense,
And bound him wi' the hempen cords
  O' plain guid sense.

"Threep as ye please, it's clear to me,
Whether or no' the twae agree,
Baith doctrines were appoint to be
  The Kirk's chief pillar.
If ane ye like to leave," says he,
  "Ye leave the siller."

Oh, wi' what unction he restored
The auld commandments o' the Lord,
Confounded Bashan's nowt that roared,
  And 'stablished Hell!
Knox was nae soonder in the Word
  Nor Calvin's sel'.

I'll no' deny yon Lowden chiel
Was gleg as ony slippery eel,
For twae-three men frae Kippenshiel
  Begood to waver;
I half inclined to doot the Deil
  A' through his claver.

But when a man o' faith and power
Uprose, he couldna bide an hour:
The weakest's doots were tided ower
    Anither towmont.
The Kirk stood firm as auld stane tower
    Wi' safe endowment.

*   *   *   *   *   *

I hae a bull, a noble breed,
A Shorthorn wi' a massy heid,
Wi' quarters fine and coat o' reid:
    On ilka lea
Frae Thurso to the banks o' Tweed
    He bears the gree.

I ca'ed him Begg, the same's his sire;
But noo for sign to a' the shire
O' yon great day when frae the mire
    Our feet we bore,
His name shall be in field and byre
    "The Chancellor."

VI

The Great War and After

Twice in the last century the Church of Scotland had made overtures to the Free Church for some form of co-operation which might lead to union, but the time was not ripe for so bold a venture. But after 1904 the atmosphere had changed, and the problem came out of the mists of idealism into the clearer air of the practicable. On the side of the Church of Scotland Archibald Scott and William Mair were the protagonists, and the leaders of the United Free Church, some of whom had been active in the old disestablishment crusade, were not slow to welcome their advances. One thing was plain: the purpose must be union or nothing, for the Churches were too closely akin for mere co-operation. A long step forward was taken in 1909, when there was a general agreement that the whole ground must be examined by unrestricted conference. Meantime two men had emerged, Dr. John White of the Church of Scotland and Dr. Alexander Martin of the United Free Church, who were to lead the movement to a triumphant conclusion; while a third, Dr. Archibald Henderson, did much to create within the latter Church the atmosphere without which union was impossible.

It is important to remember the magnitude of the task which confronted the negotiators. The field had indeed been largely cleared, but, when they began their work in 1909, the difficulties still seemed almost insuperable. One Church had been formally pledged by annual resolutions for nearly half a century to disestablishment and disendowment as a policy not only of expediency but of justice, while the other clung to the historic association with the State. It is true that many of the old lines of division had grown faint, and that the identity of the two Churches in doctrine, ritual and government had become clearer.

But this very admitted identity was in itself an obstacle. In the words of Lord Sands :

> " The differences which to a stranger seem most obscure are often the most difficult to reconcile. When two denominations are separated by some difference clear and palpable, there may be no need to justify separation. The cause is obvious. But when the difference is not of this character, it is felt that separation needs to be justified in the eyes of the world, and this leads to the attachment of immense importance to the ground of quarrel and the most tenacious and meticulous adherence to the one position or the other."

Here it is needless to trace the various steps by which the ground of difference was narrowed and the ground of agreement enlarged. The memorandum published by Lord Sands in 1912, a document which may well be called epoch-making, simplified the issue by making it clear that freedom from State control was the only possible basis of union, and that such freedom was compatible with all that the Church of Scotland valued in its relations to the State. The next step lay with the Church of Scotland, which had the task of preparing a new series of articles to declare the constitution which it regarded as its charter. It was a delicate task, and was not accomplished without controversy, but in the end it was patent that there was nothing in the creed now defined by the Church of Scotland as its basis which differed in fundamentals from that of the sister Church.

Then in August 1914 came the Great War, which proved to be the final reconciler. Co-operation there had to be, under the stress of urgent needs both in Scotland and in the field. Ministers of both communions served—after the fine Scottish fashion—not only as chaplains but as combatants, and as platoon and company commanders shed the foibles of clericalism and reached a new understanding of the ordinary man. The social duties of the Church, too often forgotten in ecclesiastical quarrels, were burned in upon such minds. The consequence was that, after the Armistice, it was found that the whole question had undergone a chemical change. The problems of reconstruction were so vast that the Church of Christ could not face them unless it possessed a united front and a unified command.

Dr. Archibald Henderson had already pointed out in 1911 the desperate needs of the new Scotland. Her population had doubled since 1843, and the two Churches did not number among their members and adherents one-half of that population. The distribution of churches was faulty, and the denominational rivalry meant a grievous waste of money and power. The two Churches between them had two hundred congregations with less than fifty members, and nearly five hundred with less than a hundred each. Moreover the War, with its urgent realities, had cast many old controversial matters still further back into the antiquarian mists. Lastly, the whole conception of the State had changed. Whig individualism had given place to a deeper and more organic conception of the part of the State in the communal life. That a Church should have some kind of relation with the civil Government no longer seemed a dereliction of Christian duty.

The new draft articles of the Church of Scotland, which were in substance akin to the old "Claim of Right," were nine in number. The first defined the faith of the Church as Trinitarian, Evangelical and Protestant, a sufficiently wide charter, and power was given to the Church to interpret the terms. The fourth, dealing with spiritual freedom, asserted in the most emphatic terms the separate and independent government and jurisdiction of the Church, and claimed the right and power to legislate, the crucial test of autonomy. The third and sixth insisted in carefully chosen words on the national recognition of religion, not as a new principle but as part of the Church's historic identity. One passage is memorable :

"This Church acknowledges the divine appointment and authority of the civil magistrate within his own sphere, and maintains its historic testimony to the duty of the nation acting in its corporate capacity to render homage to God, to acknowledge the Lord Jesus Christ as the King over the nations, to obey His laws, to reverence His ordinances, to honour His Church, and to promote in all appropriate ways the Kingdom of God. The Church and the State owe mutual duties to each other, and acting within their separate spheres may signally promote each other's welfare. The Church and the State have the right to determine each for itself all questions concerning the extent or the continuance of their mutual relations in the discharge of their duties and the obligations arising therefrom." [1]

[1] It re-echoes in parts similar declarations made in earlier times, *e.g.* the Heads of Agreement drawn up between the Free and United Presbyterian Churches in 1869, and even the Basis of Union between Burghers and Anti-Burghers in 1820.

It is a far cry from such words to the judgment of Lord President Hope, in the first Auchterarder case, that Parliament was "the temporal head of the Church, from whose acts, and from whose acts alone, it exists as a national Church, and from whom alone it derives all its powers."

The new articles were put in the form of a Bill which passed both Houses of Parliament without a division in the summer of 1921. The Act was not to come into operation till the articles had been adopted by a majority of the presbyteries of the Church of Scotland—which was accomplished by 1926. The next problem was the endowments. A commission was appointed to examine the difficult question of the teinds, ancient property rights which it was desirable to change from the position of a fluctuating annual charge to a capital sum, which could be handed over to the Church's keeping. After much negotiation an arrangement was arrived at which became the law of the land in 1925. The Church lost in the transaction nearly one-sixth of its former revenues from this source, but won complete freedom in dealing with what remained.

The Union

The Church of Scotland was now, as to creed, status and property, on the same basis as the sister Church. There remained the slow task of securing that final ratification of union from below, from presbyteries and congregations, which is an essential part of Presbyterian democracy. This task presented no difficulty in the Church of Scotland, but in the United Free Church, where there was an appreciable dissenting minority, and where the subordinate organism was more highly integrated, it required time and a patient diplomacy. In 1926 new committees were appointed in both Churches to conduct the actual negotiations, the leaders being Dr. John White and Lord Sands for the one Church, and Principal Martin and Dr. Drummond for the other. Within a year a provisional agreement was reached on a "Basis and Plan of Union," which during the next two years was carefully examined by the lower Church courts. Counsel's opinion was taken on the question as to whether, in a union with the Church of Scotland on the proposed basis, the property of the United Free Church could without breach of trust be transferred to the United Church. The present Lord Macmillan held that it could, since the Churches differed neither in creed nor ecclesiastical polity, but he advised, in order to make assurance sure, that the United Free Church should, under the terms of its constitution, expressly declare that the two Churches were at one in constitution and principle.

In the Assemblies of 1928 it was evident that the opposition, never formidable, was rapidly shrinking. The Basis of Union was sent down finally under the Barrier Act to the presbyteries, kirk-sessions and congregations being also consulted. In the Church of Scotland every presbytery voted in its favour—seventy-two out of the eighty-four unanimously. In the United Free Church all the sixty-three home presbyteries approved, and there was only a small minority of dissentients among the congregations and sessions. So at long last, in May 1929, when a royal prince acted for the first time as Lord High Commissioner, the Union was ratified by the two Assemblies. In the following October, with the Duke of York again representing the King, the first Union Assembly took place, as described in the succeeding chapter. A small minority constituted a dissenting remnant. It would not have been Scotland without such a protest.

The Hopes and Dangers of Union

"WHOSOEVER in writing a moderne Historie," Sir Walter Raleigh wrote, "shall follow truth too neare the heeles, it may happily strike out his teeth." It is not easy to judge of the ultimate value of a recent event, since it is not permitted to pry into the future. Both union and disruption have been common in our history, but romance and popular interest have attached themselves rather to the second than to the first. It is the memory of our old defiances spoken against England, the first and second Reformations, the drama of 1843, that we have been accustomed to cherish, as if our philosophy were that of Milton's famous words: "By His divorcing command the world first rose out of chaos; nor can be renewed again out of confusion but by the separating of unmeet consorts."

Yet no consort is so unmeet for the Church as antagonisms which have exhausted their justice. It is better in the long run to build up than to break down, to unite than to sever ; or, rather, destruction and severance are futile except with a view to an ultimate construction and unity. The fault of sectarianism is that it mistakes the means for the end. No doubt dissent needs courage and is often noble and justifiable, but there may be a rarer courage in an insistence upon matters of agreement rather than upon those of difference, and a stronger justification at the bar of history.

What are the dangers of union, for dangers there are ? It may involve, in Stevenson's mocking words, the

> lack of a' sectarian füsh'n,
> An' cauld religious destitution.

Human affection clings more closely to the smaller unit, as a soldier's love is for his regiment rather than for his brigade, for his division than for his corps. Particularism is apt to evoke the more strenuous loyalties.

A man's interest is keenest in what distinguishes him from the mass of his fellows, and his attachment is warmer toward those who are segregated along with himself and to the creed which segregates them. There may be a unison which is attained through a general lack of interest, a weary peace which is based not on a common faith but on a common apathy. No union is of any lasting value in which the whole does not absorb the honest loyalties formerly given to the parts. The only justification for the breaking down of particularism is a stronger faith in the fundamentals. Unless the union of the Churches is attended not merely with a freedom from contention but with a positive increase of vigour and purpose, far better was the old sectarianism. The liberty we need is Burke's liberty, " manly, moral and regulated," not a bare absence of bonds but a thing rich in content, a spirit able and eager to use its new freedom in new duties.

The circumstances in which union has been attained entitle us to hope for such a spirit. For the chief incentive to it has been a realisation of the new magnitude of the Church's problem, and the imperative demand in the face of it for the Church to free itself of encumbrances. Religious energy must be released from the obsession of lesser matters—disputes about the niceties of orthodoxy and Church government. The need to-day is for a race of prophets to arise. Scotland in the past has produced too many priests and ritualists, for there may be a deadly ritualism in a Church which abhors ritual, since the word means no more than the setting of the letter above the spirit. She has produced too many ecclesiastics who were engrossed in their own sphere, like devotees of some abstruse science, and had little regard for the uncovenanted world around them. The need to-day is for prophets who will enlarge the sphere of Christian duty and sharpen its purpose—

men to whom there is nothing secular which is not also sacred, whose antagonists are not those of their own household, who in a slightly different form profess the same faith, but the eternal enemy, sin and sorrow and pain—in the words of the Book of Revelation, "that great city which spiritually is called Sodom and Egypt, where also our Lord was crucified."

The Problems of the Christian Church

What main problems confront a united Church—confront indeed the whole Church of Christ?

There is in the first place the question of creed. Religion is not a static thing, the forms of which have been established once for all by a divine decree which admits of no fresh interpretation. It is the spiritual conception of life, and therefore of the universe in which life is lived. But it is independent of any particular cosmogony, and the old divines unfortunately were driven to make a precise cosmogony an essential article of faith. To them, if I may quote what I have written elsewhere, " the earth and all therein were made purposely by God for man, and man's journey heaven-ward or hell-ward was the sole object of creation." They held that " a few thousand years earlier the universe had been fabricated out of chaos in six calendar days, that all history antecedent to our era had been a preparation for the coming of Christ, and that, the supreme sacrifice having been accomplished, at any moment the skies might open, and the trumpets sound, and the short story of earth be closed." This cosmic assurance has crumbled before the advance of science, and to-day our view of the universe has passed far beyond such anthropocentric fancies. We see our earth, which once seemed half the cosmos, an inconsiderable planet revolving with an infinity of others in the immensity of space. We have learned that human life has relations through countless aeons with lower existences, and is kin alike to the brutes and to the stars. The universe has become stranger than any poet's dream, in the deserts of hyper-space the human mind is still blindly groping, and physical science, which a few generations ago was confident about all things in heaven and earth, now uncovers its head humbly in the presence of mysteries which it cannot fathom and can scarcely define.

In the face of this new modesty of science theology dare not be too dogmatic. We realise that it, too, is not a static thing, and that antiquarian accretions are no part of its essence. Theology is an attempt to systematise the divine revelation and to bring it into accord with every aspect of life. But life varies and enlarges its content, and the divine effluence which illuminates it must pass through new lenses. The essentials of our religion can never change. There is still for every man the choice of two paths ;

conversion in its plain evangelical sense is still the greatest fact in any life ; Bunyan's mountain gate has still to be passed, which "has room for body and soul, but not for body and soul and sin." Man must still be brought into direct communion with his Maker, and the only comfort in sorrow and pain is that he should know that his Redeemer liveth. The prime task of religion is to spiritualise life, and in this task its foe is not science and the questioning powers of the mind, for science itself is a spiritual activity. The danger comes from the application of science, which has so marvellously elaborated the mechanical apparatus of life, and may lead to an undue exaltation of mechanism. To counteract this peril there is need of a simpler and intenser evangel, freed from the lumber of a theology which itself may be a mechanical thing.

But the insistence upon the eternal simplicities of the faith will not lead us to any shallow contempt for the work of our predecessors. The doctrine of relativity holds good in this as in other spheres. A formula, which was once a potent revelation, may seem to us an empty echo, but in its own day it may have been a just and fruitful interpretation. The duty of restatement is always with us, and our own interpretation will be revised by our children. There is no discharge in the eternal struggle to adjust the spirit of man to the world by bringing his material environment within the spiritual orbit. If we seek a definition of this creed we shall find it in one who was contemporary with our own Covenanters, the Puritan Isaac Penington. "All truth," he wrote, "is shadow except the last truth. But all truth is substance in its own place, though it be but a shadow in another place. And the shadow is a true shadow, as the substance is a true substance."

Secondly, there is the problem of conduct. It is idle to deny that to-day there is a general loosening of moral sanctions, as our fathers understood them. Certain props to conventional ethics have gradually fallen away—the old tradition of church attendance, of Sabbath observance, of Bible reading. There is a good deal of moral anarchism abroad, due partly to the importance acquired by the mere mechanism of life, and partly to the popularising of half-understood philosophic doctrines about the right of each man to self-realisation and the development of the personality. The social discipline, which insisted upon a general norm of conduct, has been gravely weakened. The disintegration apparent in so much modern art and thought is not less prominent in morals.

Much of this is to the good. Pharisaism, the fidelity to conventions which have lost any binding spiritual force, is no basis for virtue. Moral sanctions need revision and adjustment as much as intellectual beliefs. Men alter their moral codes as they alter the fashion of their clothes ; witch-hunting and intolerance were once outward proofs of godliness, and slave-owning was not held to be inconsistent with humanity. The Church has the duty in such questions of facing frankly changed conditions, and bringing the light of its revelation to bear on new perplexities.

But, along with this obligation to examine problems honestly and to reject embargoes which have become meaningless, goes an obligation to insist upon the need of moral discipline—that broad, rational and humane morality which is the teaching of Christ. The revolt of young anarchy is less against Christ's mandates than against what it regards as the perversion of them by official interpreters. Disintegration is not a mood in which the world can long abide, and it is the Church's task to build up a new and wiser discipline, to " guard the fire within " though the " carved gods " have to be left behind.

It is a task which to some extent must

bring it into contact with the State, for in the present organisation of society the State must provide a legal and social background to private ethics. If on the part of the civil government there is the duty to recognise religion, there is a not less binding duty upon a national Church to advise and support the government in providing the civic sanctions for Christian morality. " I am more and more of a mind," Robert Baillie wrote, " that churchmen, be they never so abill, are unhappie statesmen " ; but there is one province of statesmanship where the Church has both the right and the duty to intervene.

In the third place, missionary enterprise has acquired in the post-war world a new meaning. It is a happy omen that the year of Union was also the centenary of the recognition by the Scottish Church of its missionary duty by the sending out of Alexander Duff to India. The development of transport and communications has brought the world closer. The War taught us that every part subtly reacts upon the rest, that all peoples are members one of another, and that the peace and prosperity of a nation may be linked organically with the peace and prosperity of remote lands. The loose, embryonic society of an older world has gone for ever, and to-day myriads of human souls depend for their very existence upon the mechanism of civilisation working in all parts of the globe with smoothness and security.

Under such conditions missionary work takes on a new meaning. It can no longer be treated as a *parergon* of the Christian Church ; it is one of its most urgent practical duties. One gain from the tragedy of war has been a recognition of the vital interest of each country in the well-being of others, however far distant in space ; and another is the slow dawning of a true internationalism, which seeks to add to the patriotisms of races and nations a patriotism of humanity. Now, world peace depends in the long run upon a universal will to peace rather than upon sanctions and treaties, upon a change of heart and a new code of values, upon the general acceptance and practice of the rules of Christian ethics. The missionary has always been the advance guard of civilisation, but to-day he is something more. He is not a lonely figure, representative of a special communion, doing his work sometimes in opposition to, generally in isolation from, the secular activities of his countrymen. He is a vital part of the new civil service of peace, and the tasks at which he labours are the same as those which from another angle are undertaken by chanceries and diplomatists. The missionary side of the Church is "established," in fact if not in law, because it works in the same province and to the same end as the civil power.

Lastly, there is the eternal problem of the society in which we live, a society which through the growth of population and the interweaving of economic interests has developed problems of infinite complexity and desperate urgency, and which reveals, along with many potentialities of hope, many dark certainties of evil. Our view of the State has moved far to-day from the old Victorian detachment. We realise that the central unity, which is the nation in its corporate character, must do more than keep the lists clear for individual effort: that it has in certain matters a direct duty, which it alone can fulfil, to supplement, and in some cases override, the private activities of its citizens. This richer conception of the State is accompanied by a quicker conscience in the individual. We no longer believe that human misery is the result of some mysterious decree of Omnipotence; we realise that it is mainly the consequence of human bungling. Nor do we consider that we can shoulder the whole burden of its relief upon any government; we recognise a personal obligation. This seems to me, among so many losses, one solid and indubitable gain. Of this duty the Church must be the inspirer and the interpreter. Its business is not only with eternity but with time, to enable men to live worthily and not merely to die in hope, and to build upon earth the Kingdom of God.

In such a task it has one prophet to show the way. Just as in the case of our greater statesmen party labels are soon forgotten, so Thomas Chalmers stands to us to-day less as the leader of the Disruption and the founder of a new Church, than as the supreme religious genius of modern Scotland. His masculine intellect made him a scholar in many spheres ; he was a famous orator and a sagacious ecclesiastic ; his character was wholly pure and benevolent, and he was as simple and modest as Sir Walter Scott. But, above all, he was that rare thing, a true national leader, who lifted his countrymen to a higher spiritual level and opened vistas that but for him had been sealed. He insisted on applying the spirit of the Evangel to the whole economy of the land. Had he been born in the days of the first Reformers he would have been as careless of his life as any, for courage was the breath of his being, but he had to deal with things more unnerving than "dag or dagger." To me he seems the greatest constructive mind that the Scottish Church has produced, and one of the noblest figures in any Church—as far above Knox in vision and wisdom as he surpassed him in charity.

Retrospect

The Church thus reunited is a new type among Christian communions, and it is right to remind ourselves of its conspicuous privileges. For the first time in history we have a Church which is acknowledged by the law of the land to be wholly free: free in its government and jurisdiction, free in its faith, having power to interpret its creeds and to alter them within the wide limits of trinitarian Protestantism, free in its use of its temporalities. And at the same time it is a historic Church, with no gap in its continuity from the first Reformers, cherishing its ancient documents of title, recognised by the State as the national representative of the faith of the Scottish people—the Church of Scotland, and not merely a Church in Scotland. The words "established" and "dis-established" have no longer any but an historical meaning. The Church is that far greater thing, a national Church, as it was in 1560 at its beginnings.

Looking back on the long story, it may well seem that no stage was without its beneficent purpose. Each schism, each controversy had its place in a great plan, for each emphasised a facet of the truth which was in danger of neglect. Men who seceded on one point gravely over-emphasised that point, but their secession and their over-emphasis secured for whatever it contained of substance a place in the national testimony. The extravagance of the seventeenth-century theocrats made it certain that no Church would ever command the assent of the Scottish people which was in spiritual bondage to the civil power, and when this article seemed in peril the eighteenth-century seceders rose to affirm it. The "voluntary" movement taught the economic side of autonomy and the importance of religious equality; those who clung to the establishment preserved the belief in a national recognition of religion. The strength of the nineteenth-century free communions gave a chance both for the liberalisation of confessions and for a larger view of the social duties of the Christian faith.

Slowly, painfully, the Church rid itself of certain sinister heritages; it shed the mediaevalism which made it a rival of the State; it abandoned its narrow Scriptural literalism ; it learned that toleration was not a pagan vice but a Christian virtue, and that the path to unity did not lie through a bleak uniformity. But all these lessons would have been vain had not a vision of the peace and felicity of a united Jerusalem survived among good men in each generation, even when their conscience demanded a further disruption. The very vigour of their scruples and their honest resolution to be loyal to what they held to be truth made it certain that unity if attained would be no shallow, unfeatured thing, but a living organism in which all that was of value in old differences would be transmuted and reconciled.

> " Why else was the pause prolonged but that singing might issue thence?
> Why rushed the discords in but that harmony should be prized? "

From the standpoint of the goal attained we can retrace the road and see how all the pilgrims, even in their deviations, contributed something to its attainment. One lightened the baggage and was cast out, but in time what he had rejected was left behind by all. Another took a course of his own in sterile country, but his followers stumbled upon Pisgah-views and returned to the main march with a new vision. Others stuck by the path which ordinary folk could travel, and formed a rallying point to unite the stragglers.

These men, moving down through the ages, are many of them great figures, attaining often to heroic stature, men who had the making of their country in their hands, for the history of Scotland is largely the history of her Church. Some are still in our memories—Rainy and Caird and Story, with faces cast in a mould of antique dignity. Behind them we see Norman Macleod with his kindly sagacity and Highland fire, and the noble head of Cunningham, and Candlish's short, gnarled figure, and John Cairns' rugged face, and Chalmers with the brow of the mathematician and the eyes of the visionary. . . . Further back are the perukes of the eighteenth century—the bland precision of Blair; the black mittens of Webster; Carlyle of Inveresk, handsome as a pagan god; the great chin and the bright, vivacious eyes of Principal Robertson; the Erskines, too, with their high foreheads and lips pursed as if in an eternal protest, and Boston of Ettrick, pale with fasting and study, and William Carstares, heavy-wigged, heavy-browed, his fingers crooked from the torture-chamber. . . . Beyond them are the men of the heather, lean, wild folk, short-lived for the most part and tragically fated, with voices shrill from hillside preaching and eyes pale like a seaman's from hilltop watches. . . . Then come the skull-caps and bands of the divines who saw their Church on the pinnacle of its temporal power—the "fair little man," half jurist, half dreamer, who was Samuel Rutherford, and Alexander Henderson, his skin yellow with ague and his eyes hollow with unsleeping thought, a statesman born in an ill season for statesmanship. . . . Now we are among the flat caps of the Reformers, chief of them Knox with his hawk's nose and hawk's eye and patriarch's beard, the man who had the passionate momentum of some great portent of nature. . . . Then the mists descend, and we see only dim figures in proud hieratic robes, and sometimes under the robes a gleam of steel, for they were often of the church militant, and served in the field as well as at the altar. . . . But in the far distance the air clears, and against a Hebridean sky we can discern him who was called the Dove and was both priest and prince, and who on another isle, like John on Patmos, had visions of a peace among men which " has its birth in mortal love, but its evening home where are the dews of immortality."

VII

Postscript: The Kirk since 1929

The reunion of the Church of Scotland had created a very large Kirk of some 1·3 million members, with nearly half the adult population of Scotland in formal communicant membership. It had, for the first time since the eighteenth century, gathered the vast majority of Scots Protestants into the one Church organisation. It had created a formula by which the Kirk could profess to be a National Church without being a State Church. But it had not restored the Kirk to the place in Scottish life which it had once held. Scotland was not insulated from the secularising influences that affected almost all Europe. In some ways it was also less distinct in its cultural identity than ever before. The Scots of the 1930's listened to the BBC, often read newspapers controlled in

Fleet Street, and wondered if H. G. Wells and George Bernard Shaw were more significant prophets than those of the Old Testament. Church reunion had failed to solve three problems—or what seemed to be problems—of which the leaders of the Kirk were very conscious.

They laced their oratory with evangelical calls about reaching the "churchless million". Even in 1929 the figure may have underestimated the problem. To read between the lines is to discover that many of those leaders appreciated the extent to which a large section of the Protestant working class had stayed outside formal Church membership, even if it still wanted its children to go to Sunday school. But it was, and has remained, easier to identify that problem than to reverse the trends.

Secondly, there were signs that the reunited Kirk realised how far large sections of the middle class, even nominal church members, were drifting from the habits of regular churchgoing, never mind evangelical commitment. Cars, golf, hiking, and the cinema were changing social patterns. So was radio—even when the BBC was run by a son of the Scottish manse, John Reith, in London and a minister, Melville Dinwiddie, in Scotland.

There was a third problem which the Kirk was intensely aware of in the 1930's. Roman Catholicism was gaining in numbers, now more by natural growth than by immigration, and deepening its penetration in political, economic and social matters, however slowly. From 1918, for example, Scots Roman Catholics had a separate state-financed educational system, much more congenial to them than the State schools offered in many Catholic countries. It was resented by many Protestants. The Scotland of the inter-war years, long before Rome's interest in the ecumenical movement, had a strong sectarian consciousness—most marked in the West of Scotland but not confined to it—in which the old theological differences were compounded by the bitterness of the Irish struggle for independence. As John Buchan made one of his wartime characters say in *Mr. Standfast*, "Glasgow's stinkin' nowadays with two things, money and Irish". After the war there was not so much money about, but there was a Scottish Protestant resentment of Irish-descended Catholicism.

Yet in many ways the immediate post-reunion years were a time of achievement and initiative in the Kirk. The long process euphemistically called "union and readjustment" had begun. This meant closing some of the churches which were immediately and obviously redundant when the halves of Presbyterianism came together again. Even before 1929 the U. F. Kirk probably had too many churches for its separate existence, being itself a union of the Free and United Presbyterian traditions. Inevitably, disproportionate energy was perhaps channelled both into the official pressures for rationalisation and into the countless local rear-guard actions against closures.

More constructively, the reunited Kirk successfully coped through its Church Extension Scheme with providing churches for council and other new housing areas. There was enough money in the 1930's to build the kirks in stone and with modest architectural pretensions—even sometimes in a curiously hybrid, but effective, mixture of Scots and North European style: a kind of Hanseatic Baronial.

There was also the urge to give the Gospel social expression. The Tory Buchan wanted the Church to be inspirer and interpreter of Christian social values at a time when "we have a richer and broader conception of the State". When such a Tory put deliberate emphasis on the social reforming streak in Thomas Chalmers and John Wesley it is not surprising that less conservative churchmen explored new forms of radicalism and preached a social Gospel which at times merged into a Socialist Gospel. In doing so they were challenging both the secular and anti-clerical streak in Socialism (Keir Hardie notwithstanding), and the middle-class support for the "National" Government mood of the 1930's.

John Buchan hankered after a curious kind of Christian hero whom he called the "Presbyterian cavalier". His obvious example was the seventeenth-century Royalist Covenanter, the Marquis of Montrose, though he added Stonewall Jackson, and perhaps less convincingly, Douglas Haig.

But in the age of depression urban Scotland was still struggling with the evil consequences of the industrial revolution, without the consolations of industrial expansion. A small but dedicated group of Scots—most notably John Maclean—were more attracted to commissars than Covenants, though Clydeside was never as red as it was painted. Scottish Socialism had both an anti-clerical and a Christian reforming tradition (including a Roman Catholic one associated with John Wheatley) and in the climate of the times attracted even the latest of the Presbyterian cavaliers—and that even rarer gallant, the pacifist cavalier.

The dominant constructive statesman of the inter-war Kirk was John White. The most powerful radical influence was George MacLeod, grandson of White's greatest predecessor at the Barony, Norman Macleod, and founder of the Iona Community. Although the restoration of the abbey there was an integral part of MacLeod's concept, his vision of a radicalised Church owed more to his ministry in Govan, a shipyard area of Glasgow especially hard hit by the depression.

Pacifism went in MacLeod's case with a rather individualistic Socialism. In the case of another ex-officer also awarded an M.C., Archie Craig, it was even more distant from the politics of the class-war. But there was a much broader pacifist or at least pacific movement in the Kirk, which probably owed more to the Liberal tradition that had been strong in the U. F. Kirk. Between the wars this powerful group was strongly inclined towards the League of Nations. Actual pacifism never became the dominant opinion of the Kirk, but perhaps — combining with a much more conservative mood—it managed to delay its response to the real threat of war and its realisation of the nature of the menace emerging in Hitler's Germany.

Angry words and strong passions can still be roused among the survivors of these years by suggestions that the Kirk was slow to identify itself with the Confessing Church in Germany or to break the academic links, which had partly been restored after the First World War, with the German universities, even after they had been reconstructed to the satisfaction of the Third Reich. Karl Barth attracted some very able young scholars from the Kirk—Tom Torrance notably—but he failed to establish a close rapport with some of the Scots theologians who had worldwide influence, especially the Baillies.

There was even a tendency at first—quite apart from a few eccentrics who were misled by the "German Christian movement"—to hope that the Nazi revolution was a temporary rush of blood to the head and that in time things in Germany would settle down. It was possible for some conservative people (unprepared for the later alliance of Hitler and Stalin) to see Nazism merely as a kind of nationalism with a bee in its bonnet about the Jews and a weakness for dressing up in uniform.

But not for long. If the Kirk was slow to respond to the persecution of the Jews it was because it saw Nazism as just another manifestation of the kind of anti-Semitism in Hungary or Poland or Romania which had become depressingly familiar. It soon became clear that German Jews—including "non-Aryan" Christians—faced something even worse. The Scots Church took an honourable stand and with limited resources gave what help it could in Prague and Budapest to many people who had to leave Germany. Several refugees eventually settled into its ministry, enriching it with such un-Scottish names as Ehrlich and Citron.

War came with fewer heroics this time, and perhaps more questions about why God allowed it than assertions about what he wanted done in it. But there was a solemn commission to find God's will for Church and Nation, which worked under the convenership of John Baillie. Presbyterians expect a lot from committees!

There were "days of prayer", sermons about the marvellous weather at Dunkirk, and services on V.E. Day at which the Old 124th ("Now Israel may say . . .") was sung just as heartily as in 1918. There was even a minister who secured the largest radio audience that anyone in the Kirk had ever known till that time—perhaps larger than any Scots minister was ever to achieve again. Ronald

Selby Wright, temporarily moved from the Canongate to a Royal Scots battalion, found a niche and a knack as the Radio Padre in an age when everyone not only listened to the radio, but to the same thing.

The First World War cracked the foundations of the Western World in which the Church had exercised a great moral, social, and intellectual power. The Church emerged weaker, and perhaps more weakened than it realised. The Second World War had a different impact and seemed, if anything, to strengthen the Church. The ministry was refreshed by a large crop of ex-Servicemen. Membership remained stable. After the war Western humanity seemed chastened by the demonstration of how far technological skill had outrun the capacity to use and control it.

Perhaps there was also one of those blessed times when theology, preaching, evangelism, pastoral care, and social concern seemed to be in harmony. There was much indirect influence, even in the ordinary parish sermon, of Karl Barth, Reinhold Niebuhr, and William Temple. Barth contributed new insights to biblical theology, in particular the Word, the doctrine of grace, and the centrality of Christ that suited the traditions and temperament of Scots Presbyterianism. Niebuhr and Temple seemed superb tractarians for the times. Of the native theologians the most eminent and important (at least until Tom Torrance achieved an international reputation) was John Baillie, though his brother Donald had that indefinable influence of a great teacher who wrote relatively little. John Baillie, who convened the wartime commission "for the interpretation of God's will", was a Christian apologist who arranged a successful marriage of theology and practical piety. He also expressed as clearly as anyone the early, unclouded optimism of the ecumenical movement.

Perhaps it was the mood of the peace, with its frustrations, austerity, and demonstrations that dictatorship had not died in

Hitler's bunker, that made the Church in Western Europe a pillar of a society in which many of the other pillars had crumbled. It took the lead in coping with Europe's scattered millions of refugees and displaced persons. In Germany, with help from other churches, it began the restoration of Christian contacts even when the official occupation line was "non-fraternisation". Surprisingly soon, some of the old links with German theology were restored or revived—often through personal contacts and even family connections—and took new forms. (Today, for example, there is a Scot holding a chair in Reformed theology in the mainly Lutheran faculty at Erlangen.) And in 1948 a bright day dawned (or so it seemed) with the creation of the World Council of Churches. The Church of Scotland was deeply involved in the accompanying mood of internationalism and ecumenism. As Buchan had in 1929, it felt that the different streams of Christendom were flowing into a desert in need of their reviving power.

At home the Kirk resumed the considerable movement of Church Extension that had been suspended during the war and its immediate aftermath. Ministers found many people who moved house ready to resume a church connection that had lapsed; even those reluctant to cross the church door remained interested in the Sunday schools (and even more the youth organisations) for their children.

There was a new burst of evangelistic enthusiasm to reassure those who feared this active Kirk might be spiritually lifeless. The evangelicals enthused over Billy Graham, and most of those who could not enthuse very much had the grace to hold their peace. Ronald Falconer of the BBC, a superb broadcaster for whom religious broadcasting was the "handmaid of the Church", linked this evangelical enthusiasm to a Radio Mission.

Scotland found another very attractive

evangelical saint with an intense social conscience in a Glasgow minister called Tom Allan, who was at the heart of the *Tell Scotland* movement. Briefly there was even a "Kirk Week" movement which looked as if it might give Scotland some of the lay enthusiasm of the German Protestant *Kirchentag*. It flickered and faded.

In 1960 the Kirk laid on its most spectacular event since 1929, at a special General Assembly to mark the fourth centenary of the Scottish Reformation, this time with a visit from the sovereign herself.

But suddenly things began to go wrong. The 1950's turned out to be a high peak for the Kirk that was reunited in 1929. By the 1960's there had begun a long, slow decline that (at least statistically) shows no sign of halting even in the mid-1980's. In 1956 the Kirk's membership was a post-war (perhaps all-time) peak of nearly 1,320,000. By 1984 it was 902,000. It had fallen every year since 1956, at first very slowly, then quite markedly. Of course this was not an isolated phenomenon for the Kirk. Similar trends began at about the same time to affect many other Western Churches, not least English-speaking mainstream denominations. Five phenomena which were found in Scotland—sometimes taking distinctive forms—had their parallels in other countries:

First, there was an ecumenical failure (or stalemate) among the Protestant Churches, followed by a fitful and at times confused response to the quite different ecumenical momentum generated by the Roman Catholic Church after the impact of Pope John XXIII. The Church decided it did not want bishops-in-the-Kirk (as a major report had proposed), finding the Anglicans could not accept unity without episcopacy. But it was now inhibited about expressing Protestant feelings frankly, and seemed uncomfortable rather than hostile or welcoming when Pope John Paul II visited Scots Roman Catholics in 1982.

Second, there was a polarisation of opinion, style and priorities, not only in theology and liturgy, but to some extent in political and social matters. Clearly some energetic groups in the Kirk had more in common with kindred spirits in other denominations than with each other.

It is possible, for example, to wax enthusiastic about liturgical developments or evangelical initiatives in the Kirk—see almost any volume of the Blue Book of reports to the General Assembly—with scant appreciation of how few congregations may have been profoundly affected by either, or how widely the energetic minorities may differ in style from each other. In the long run this may help to keep the Kirk national and comprehensive and to meet many tastes and needs. It may also widen the range of its ecumenical contacts, from salvationists to liberationists. But it can make the pilgrim Presbyterian uncertain at times whether he is in the Delectable Mountains or back in

Vanity Fair. Where there have been changes on a wider front—for example an increase in the number of Communion services and a stronger emphasis on the "Christian Year" (especially Christmas)—it is not always clear that the changes have proved as significant as their advocates expected.

Third, there was a reflection in and by the Kirk of social, economic, and political confusion and unease in Scotland. The years of Church decline coincided with economic decay in Scotland's heavy industries and with the political trends which moved Scotland leftwards with spasms of nationalist and devolutionist enthusiasm. (Just how confused the Kirk itself could be was shown in the obvious division within it at the 1979 devolution referendum.)

Fourth, there was a problem of leadership. Somehow the times did not seem to summon up another John White or a successor to George MacLeod. There seemed to be few Presbyterian cardinals—or cavaliers!

The fifth point is arguable. But the traditions, styles and structures of Scots Presbyterianism may have made it even more vulnerable than some other churches in the face of the crisis of authority which was one aspect of the generation gap which opened up in the 1960's. It had neither the elasticity of Roman Catholicism nor (on the whole) the absolute and blessed assurance of, say, the Baptists.

From the 1960's onwards the biggest single cause of the Kirk's statistical decline was quite simply that deaths were running at roughly twice the number of new admissions by "profession of faith". In the years between 1964 and 1975 annual admissions on such professions declined from 33,000 to less than 14,000—steadying thereafter but never recovering and still tending to slip downward. In the same years there were drastic falls in Sunday school rolls and a steady fall (to under 30 per cent in 1984) in the proportion of Scots children baptised in the Kirk.

Even when the Kirk was flexible, far-sighted, and efficient in tackling its problems—as it was in accepting women's ordination to ministry and eldership in the 1960's—it got little credit for it, either in Scotland or the World Church. It worried about its worship going stale, but learned (sometimes the hard way) that neither ecumenical nor liturgical experiments have much appeal to the absent member and the determinedly unattached. It discovered that many of its most vigorous congregations (and there are thriving parishes in very varied Scottish settings) were conservative in both their style and their theology.

Yet this active, and in some things atypical, minority cannot effectively reach the majority of Scots. Only at the graveside, or more often now by the unseen fiery furnace, is the Kirk still in any definable sense the religious institution of the Scottish people. If it is still a spiritual home, in less definable senses, it is often unvisited and at times in visible spiritual ill-repair.

Its arguments and announcements on matters ecumenical or economic can still command a fair degree of media attention in Scotland—and, when it finds itself admitting a murderer and an embezzler to its ministry, far beyond Scotland. The same publicity is guaranteed when a president of the Woman's Guild calls God "Mother". Perhaps some things now taken for granted in ecumenical Geneva still sound more shocking in a Scottish accent.

To the liberals, never mind the radical theologians of liberation, the Kirk often seems staid, parochial, and inward-looking. To a new wave of conservative evangelicals it can seem timid and compromising, or too ready to be diverted into arguments about matters of secondary importance—such as an elder or minister experiencing a soaking at a "second baptism". Probably there has been a trickle of evangelicals from the Kirk into other groups or denominations, though a growing minority of its diminished ministry and membership might be classed as evangelical and even fundamentalist. The most significant trends in the Kirk are not always those that command most publicity or capture the committee structure.

Today the Kirk is hard put to it to know whether its diversity is a source of weakness or strength. Its Presbyterian system conceals differences at least as wide as those of the more obvious parties in other denominations. Even a new disruption is not altogether unthinkable. Just conceivably, it could be produced by some quarrel over the Divinity faculties—where Church influence is now much diluted and what remains is sometimes ultra-liberal; or over some new twist to the now familiar attempts to sort out the confusion over doctrinal standards and "the substance of the faith". Less improbably, it could be provoked if the ecumenical party ever gets within sight of success in the bid to accept episcopacy for the sake of unity.

But in the decades ahead the Kirk is likely to hold together, suffer further fits of trembling and convulsion, and rattle some increasingly dry bones.

All the same, the dry bones will hear the Word of the Lord, as in the great vision of Ezekiel. And there will be new sinew and flesh, breath and life. "And ye shall know that I am the Lord".

So at least it must seem to the faithful.

There is much in the life of the Kirk as well as the character of Scottish people and the history of the country to make such a vision possible. There are high tides and ebb tides in the history of the Church.

And there is no other religious institution or structure that can provide for the needs of the Scottish people. Indeed over the greater part of the territory of Scotland the National Church remains the only denomination in touch with the life of the community and within reach of everyone. Accessibility, not doctrine or style of worship, has brought new members in many a scattered parish from Anglicans, or Baptists, or even agnostics with second thoughts, who have no other available expression of religious need and pastoral service. The pattern in the cities, and especially industrial Clydeside, is very different. There are areas where the Kirk seems to run a poor third to paganism and Roman Catholicism: but it survives, and survival means potential revival.

This is not quite the picture the Kirk's Boards and Presbyteries would like to paint. They claim, justly enough, that they maintain a substantial range of social work, not just filling in gaps of public provision but often pioneering ahead of it. They trot the Moderator of the day round coal mines and fish farms. They profess all the fashionable concerns such as racism, sexism, and arms control. They take pride in trying to raise more money, pay ministers better, or close another couple of hundred churches with struggling congregations in the hope (not always fulfilled) that the remaining congregations will be stronger. They struggle to match the old missionary spirit in an age of "partner Churches".

But no-one in the Kirk is foolish enough to think that the view from Heaven necessarily coincides with the view from the Church offices in George Street, a miniature Vatican without a Pope.

Given that the world escapes nuclear oblivion, the future of the Kirk depends on the revival of the West and the survival of Christianity in a way that makes Creeds and Confessions affirm its unity rather than confirm its divisions. It depends on Scotland, which so happily combined the missionary urge with the imperialist, finding a reasonably contented place in a Europe happily aligning unity and nationality.

Just conceivably, the Kirk will ultimately become, in a political as well as a true spiritual sense, a province of the universal Church. There could be something approaching visible unity, with bishops that mean different things to different Christians and a Grand Synod Convener whom some call the Vicar of Christ. More likely, the Kirk will become even more influenced than today by currents of opinion and styles in worship that cut across the old denominational, confessional, national, and cultural lines. The General Assembly will respond to new prophets in Brazil or Indonesia—no more suprising, perhaps, than that it should once have been influenced indirectly by an itinerant Anglican horseman called John Wesley, or even more directly by an earlier French intellectual. It is harder to see the Kirk today as Scotland's "natural leader"—in Buchan's phrase—and only just possible still to insist on his claim that Presbyterianism is Scotland's most "idiomatic possession".

Even his eagerness to see the Scots Kirk as

a "bridge church" is harder to emulate today. Today those who play at ecclesiastical bridge-building are far more ambitious, if far less skilled or realistic. They want bridges between Christianity and Marxism, never mind Rome and Reform. Buchan's plausible desire was to see his Kirk, so "resolute both to discard and to retain", as the bridge between the Churches rich in historic accretions and the Churches which lack them. (He probably meant mainly the Church of England and the Free Churches.) That role has been taken by modern Lambeth and the World Council of Churches in Calvin's Geneva, even by the progressives and liberation theologians in communion with Rome. The bridges may not be safe to walk on, but there are plenty of designs for them. And the Christians lacking "historic accretions" have either decayed or regrouped. The Kirk is scarcely a bridge at the moment to new movements like Pentecostalism, or to the Baptists.

Much that was valuable in the Scottish tradition of worship and theology has been scattered as good seed through many other countries and Churches. Now and again a Scots voice or prose style (or both, as in the case of William Barclay) will communicate effectively round the English-speaking world, and even in England itself.

Barclay must rank high among the century's Christian communicators. There are others among his Scottish contemporaries and successors who have built up an international reputation and influence, though perhaps the outstanding theologian among them, Tom Torrance, is as contrasting a kind of Christian communicator as anyone could imagine. (His work on the relation of what he calls "natural and theological science" brought him the Templeton Prize for Progress in Religion.) There are also Scots university teachers who seem to command greater influence on their lecture tours abroad than in the affairs of their own

Church. The Scottish role in the world Church (however diminished since the Edinburgh International Missionary Conference of 1910 or the early days of the W.C.C.) is still significant and quite out of proportion to Scotland's population or its present political and economic influence.

Yet perhaps for the moment the Kirk must survive and then revive as that "most idiomatic possession of Scotland"; and once revived will be an effective bridge—helping to link the institutional Church with the freshness and spontaneity of new evangelical movements, continuing to link Britain to continental European culture and traditions, maintaining many of the links that have been under strain since the passing of the Empire and the old missionary enthusiasm.

A national Church must always beware of being drawn into an idiom which owes more to nationality than Christianity. The Kirk has to guard against the danger without over-reacting to it. It sometimes finds that things it takes for granted strike strangers as valuable and enviable—for example the involvement (to quote an English professor in a Scots divinity faculty) "in the political and civic life of the community in true Reformation tradition". For history and nationality have made Scots Presbyterianism distinct in its style from all other Reformed Churches, sometimes very obviously, sometimes very subtly. But Presbyterianism has given Scots Christianity a different texture from that of Scandinavia or England. Neither the country nor the Kirk is comprehensible except in relation to each other.

That will remain true whatever the future holds for them.

What Buchan wrote more than half a century ago remains valid: "Without some understanding of the Church there can be no true understanding of Scottish history or of the nature of the Scottish people."